Riding the Wave

The adventure towards
the Transpersonal

STEFANO PISCHIUTTA

ISBN: 1546324895
ISBN-13: 978-1546324898

Cover:
Transition, by Meletios Meletiou
www.meletiosmeletiou.com
(courtesy of the artist)

Graphics: Elena Antoniadou

To those who ride a higher wave

Contributing to the healthy growth
of the people who are entrusted to me:
this is my current duty in life

INDEX

INTRODUCTION

When I was twenty years old, I worked as a laborer in a metal nets factory.

That experience had been so meaningful to me that, when I finally left the factory, I decided that one day I would have recounted my story.

But, because at the time I was very young and didn't feel living up to a task that I considered very difficult, having as my models *The Betrothed* by Alessandro Manzoni and *The Master and Margarita* by Mikhail Bulgakov, it took many years – about fifteen – to find the courage to put on paper what I judged an incredible experience. And I succeeded.

So, I contacted a literary critic in order to have the manuscript evaluated, before proposing it to various publishers. Her feedback on the "novel" was inflexible: the composition was trivial, because there was no acme in it, it was written in first person and was full of superfluous, if not useless, details. On the whole, it would have never worked. Disappointed, I abandoned the project.

Only ten years later, I found the courage to self-publish the book, whose title, from the initial "Quattro anni in fabbrica" ("Four years at the factory") I changed in "Manuel e gli altri" ("Manuel and the others") (www.lulu.com). I had rewritten some parts and of course I had followed some of the helpful hints given by the critic, but I hadn't changed the first person in the story, because I wanted to talk about me and didn't want to have another talking about me with the fictitious voice of a character.

Of course, it's hard not to talk about oneself when one wants to share a personal experience with a possible audience. By the same token, it is true that it makes no sense to write a novel that talks about oneself; a work of art must be as universal as possible and the artist ought to be able to "mention without saying."

In introducing the present book, which certainly is not a novel nor a work of art, I want to restate that the topics treated in it are an outcome of my experience, as well as of my studies; therefore, I know them firsthand.

The book is about states and stages of consciousness. As a consequence, it can be better understood by those who have been living or have intuited such states and stages. In particular, it describes difficulties and challenges faced by anyone who is trying to go beyond the average level of human development, adaptation, the so-called *conventional* level.

At this stage of development, wherein most people dwell, one cannot live a really satisfying, vibrant life, fully expressing one's own potential. In short, one cannot be creative.

Whoever aspires to a creative life and to genuinely evolve must confront the limits, present in himself and in the others. This confrontation is of paramount importance for one's success, it's a crucial factor in it. In fact, our success is totally dependent on how we relate to limits, that is, on our ability to recognize and accept them, then eventually trying to overcome them.

We should understand that the stage of development (and of consciousness) wherein we dwell at a given moment of our life depends on the type of needs and motivations that drive us at that moment, just as it's true that if we reach a higher degree of development our needs and motivations change.

While waiting for their evolution to happen, however, we should learn to listen to our needs and satisfy them. We should balance them when they are in conflict with one another, in order to give them the right space in our lives.

Having vs. being is the basic conflict of human nature. Used as we are to rely on certainties, we become experts in acquiring, that is, having; but then, since we have a spiritual nature, we are pushed to fulfil our potential in being.

Are we able to let the two thrusts be, fully aware that we want the "having" withdraw in favour of "being", or do we hold a position of dependence on possessions, completely forgetting our true purpose in life, which is to evolve and develop our deepest potential? This conflict, if it's not solved, or at least treated, prevents us from growing.

In the path towards growth, our initial decision to undertake the work, whose outcome is uncertain, is crucial, and that decision means "getting on the wave." In doing so, we put ourselves in the direction of working on our resistances to growth.

Most people, though they are attracted by the charm and beauty of this path, remain in the position of observers, merely witnessing the growth of others, whom they may admire, but never trying to imitate them by standing on their own feet.

Our inner nature, whose essence is ultimately spiritual, calls us to grow beyond the level of the ordinary ego. And this call can take place even though the psychological conflicts in our personality are scarcely resolved. Anyway, we should unravel them, if we want to remain on the wave and not surrender immediately, running down it.

The surrender easily ensues from discouragement, that is, from our strong tendency to not taking responsibility for our failures and incapabilities, laying them instead onto others or onto life. All this happens, ultimately, for the simple purpose of defending an idealized image we have of ourselves. This internal dynamic lies at the core of narcissism.

Another temptation to leave the wave is represented by conformism, the adherence to a collective image of the correct being and behaving.

In cultivating the being needs there is no certainty; therefore, one must navigate at sight, in an ocean of uncertainty. But the search for safety – which once came from cultivating our deficiency needs, the ones derived from the "having" attitude – is now replaced by the deepening of intuition: we sense the truth, even though we still cannot see it clearly.

We can no longer depend on others, but we have to tap into the treasure abiding within us, that we have to discover in order to pull out our potential, left dormant for so long.

Furthermore, in this path some difficulty arises that we never suspected could possibly exist. Doubt, fear of isolation, weariness, these are all difficulties we go through in resisting the request for leaving the predominance of our ideal image of ourselves, by which we feel special individuals making a special path.

Our shadows come easily into the open when we try to overcome limits never reached before and the denial to recognise that we have a substratum of anger, fear and pain, turns into expectations that things go according to our plans. If our expectations are not realized, we become disappointed. Disappointment is perhaps the biggest risk that meets he who has got on the wave and is firmly stabilized on it.

So, in order not be overwhelmed by frustrated expectations, it can be very useful to live as if one were always a beginner, even though it is not true actually. If we feel always beginners, however, we can cultivate the aspect of curiosity, the love for discovery and the study of new topics, or topics already known but from a new perspective

Finally, curiosity can be brought into the path of growth by conceiving this path as a study of oneself. Another antidote to the frustrated

16

expectations is amusement; namely, living one's commitments, duties and interests as if one were a happy and safe child. It's difficult, but not impossible. In addition, we may learn to let ourselves go to the events, adverse as they could be, offering no resistance. Believing in God can help us in this regard, because if we believe we know what really means to surrender to God.

In addition to the difficulties described above, undertaking the path of interiority often brings with itself an unexpected guest: loneliness. Perhaps for the first time in our life we truly realize that we are alone. For those who have got on the wave, loneliness is both a condemnation and a blessing.

It is a condemnation for the part of the ego that still needs to be reassured and it is a blessing for the healthy part of the ego that aims at evolving. Loneliness consciously sought brings creativity; silence is essential for creativity; therefore, loneliness accompanying silence is fundamental too.

Ultimately, we should take into account that our life runs on two parallel tracks: a psychological dimension, represented by ego, our personality, which is expressed by its characteristics and peculiarities; a spiritual dimension, which is regarded in transpersonal psychology as a centre of consciousness, called *Self*, the spiritual essence that abides in the heart of all beings, particularly investigated by Jung (the father of analytical psychology) and Assagioli (the founder of psychosynthesis). The Self operates on the basis of universal and synthetic principles, and guides the ego.

Hence, we can live our life staying on the first track and ignoring the second, or recognizing the second as predominant on the first one. The quality of our existence and the ability to face its challenges and events depends on which of the two options we choose as predominant.

The adventure towards the transpersonal (transpersonal means, literally, "beyond ego"), that is, the path that we undertake to evolve beyond the constraints of the ego, should be a progressive experience, in which we gradually train ourselves to die – an initiatory death, of course, the death of the ego – in order to move closer to a deeper, and more authentic, inner dimension.

Transpersonal psychology in its integral approach (founded by Ken Wilber, the American philosopher of consciousness, and carried forward in Italy by the psychologist Laura Boggio Gilot) has got the right tools for helping people overcome the various evolutionary steps that lead from ego to Self, wherein psychological and spiritual difficulties of all kinds can arise, manifesting themselves as resistances, idealizations, reconsiderations.

Do we want to be heroes in our life or let life overwhelm us? Is this question important for us and how do we try to answer it? Do we think it is a matter reserved for some chosen few, so we renounce to ask it? Or we believe that it concerns all of us? Certainly, this is a challenge that concerns all of us, we are all born to evolve, that is, ultimately, to "ride the wave."

1
LIMITS

Earthly life is undoubtedly made of limits. That's a fact. Therefore, since its origin, humanity has always sought to overcome them. If we reflect well, any attempt, that to which we tend, from the very first moment of our existence, consists in trying to overcome the limitations imposed by nature.

This is somehow part of our DNA. If we relinquish our daily effort to overcome our limits, we prevent from expressing ourselves, from creating, building and, ultimately, we renounce our own lives.

Life is movement, by which we tend to move from less to (hopefully) more favourable situations. Our own evolution consists necessarily in overcoming obstacles and limits. A new acquaintance, a new discovery, in its newness involves passing a limit that initially seemed impassable. The result of the newness is a sense of satisfaction, completeness, activity and happiness. Billion people on our planet go to sleep hoping they will feel they have passed some limit. Ultimately, it looks like passing limits is one of the main tasks of our existence.

The desire for creativity is inherent in the human being. Animals and other life forms probably act on an instinctual basis; they don't desire but seek to achieve the best adaptation to their environment, for reproductive and conservative purposes. Unlike all the other life forms, and for this reason inferior to us, we humans have, in addition to reproduction and conservation, the goal of creativity.

Besides, we wish to conquer, since creating means conquering the secrets of nature, hidden from our sight. Sometimes we exaggerate with our desire for conquest and the creative drive turns into a destructive one; just think of the wars for the conquest of territories and the subjugation of peoples (often in the name of religion or civilization), that the human beings have never stopped doing.

Essentially, with the good, which is inherent in the creation, we come to know evil, that is, destruction. What in nature occurs only for adaptive purposes and objectives, then responding to universal laws, in humans is subjected to personal will, both individual and collective.

So, unlike other forms of life, that are driven by instinct, thus responding spontaneously to nature requirements, we often stray from these requirements and, having free will, in creating we often place ourselves in opposition to natural laws. Still, whether we do good or we do evil, we always respond to an interior creative drive, that comes from our inner depths. Simply, sometimes we misunderstand the meaning of that drive, thus producing evil.

Certainly, we are not called to evil, but evil is a result of a badly directed will, that drives us to carry out actions in contradiction to the laws of order and harmony. So, in trying to overcome the limits we can produce both good and evil. Ultimately, our deepest drive, in every action and intention we have, consists in overcoming all the limits that separate us from our innermost nature, the Self.

We have got limits in relation to external reality, because we live in a collective context, thereby in expressing ourselves we must necessarily take into account the other humans and the environment surrounding us. In short, we must first learn and then abide by the rules established by our community. This protects ours and other peoples' survival and existence.

The enormous effort made by man so far has been the one to achieve a high level of civilization, or adaptation to a life meant as being inserted in a social context. Man cannot survive alone, but neither in a small clan. Our current collective cognitive level requires us to be organized in societies and, more specifically, in Nations and States; at present, democracy is arguably the most advanced sociopolitical form.

Some may feel that this type of organization is limited, but there is no doubt that it ensures a higher standard of living than other types of organizations. Perhaps, as some are claiming, the Internet will bring gradually to new forms of government for societies; probably, they will still be democracies, but with additional, more advanced, participative modalities.

Maybe, who knows, it's too early to speculate about the future, while it is still so difficult to interpret correctly the current events, in a reality that changes daily, with astonishing speed, and that often seems unpredictable.

In short, at a collective level we have internalized the importance of respecting the limits in order to live well adapted and dismiss ghosts that in the past have caused collective destruction, such as war, famine, epidemics.

However, it's true that a large proportion of the inhabitants of our planet has not yet reached this level of evolution, and much of what has been said so far refers mainly to the so-called western world. And it's equally true that this western world is likely to return to pre-industrial levels, if problems such as global warming and the exploitation of non-renewable energies, as well as the world's overpopulation and scarcity of drinking water are not seriously faced. Actually, all these problems are bound to lead to catastrophic consequences for the entire planet.

In an atmosphere of good adaptation, then, humanity can dedicate its energies for the sake of its own growth. Humanity evolves not only because it acquires opportunities for a greater *comfort*, a more secure existence, a healthier and longer life, but also because it can grow in awareness. Therefore, the overall level of mankind's evolution is the result and the mirror of the evolutionary level of the average individual.

A person's level of evolution results in her level of consciousness. This latter represents the quantity and quality of facts of the existence the person is aware of.

Leaving aside here the sociological, economic and political analysis of the global problems related to the limits in the external reality, let's go inside our interiority, where we encounter limits that prevent us from living and evolving in awareness. Even they, as the outer ones, exist in some way to ensure survival and adaptation, to our internal environment in this case.

The relationship with these limits develops itself during infancy; throughout the first 3 years, roughly, we learn the essential basics that allow us to get acquainted with the existence of the limits. Basically, we come to understand that we may have a limited control over reality and that we exist in a world where our freedom is conditioned by the one of others and by the structure of the environment wherein we live.

We learn this notion basically by upbringing; in particular, by the one given by the parental system. Both in case of excessive limits imposed by this system and in case we have no imposition at all, we can have, during our growth, enormous difficulties, both in the relational field and in self-assertiveness, not to mention in the acceptance of frustrations.

In childhood we would need someone to teach us what are the proper limits, so that we can learn to relate properly to the limits imposed by reality and subsequently to our own limits. If we don't experiment the limits in childhood, it will be far more difficult to do it in adulthood. Then, probably we won't even recognize them; or, if we get in touch with them, we will hardly accept them.

Can we recognize that there are some limits within us? Do we feel that we have no limit or maybe we feel so limited to the point that we cannot even take autonomous initiatives in our life? If we can answer these questions, we can start to establish a healthy relationship with ourselves.

Some might argue at this point: "Well, I am a unified person; how am I supposed to have a relationship with someone in me different from the one who I feel I am? I can certainly put myself in connection with another, but not with myself. There isn't in me anyone different from the one whom I already am. What's all this? It's just mental trash ..."

These considerations conceal a deception in which we easily fall when we think naively to be whole within us by the mere fact that we are able to think and judge. Unfortunately, it is not so, but it is still not easy to surrender to this fact of life.

We should get used to seeing our inner world as something totally unknown and unfinished, made in layers, as is the Earth. Using this metaphor (and all we know that it's impossible to get to the center of the Earth), we can only vaguely imagine how difficult it can be to get to the center of ourselves. It's really quite an impossible mission.

Of course, the more we go in depth the more we find contents to be explored, but even remaining on the surface we have interesting things to see and on which to work. This inner work makes our life really interesting and full and, even only for this reason, it is worth doing it.

Our truest essence lies within our core, in the depths of our being, as it is claimed by all authentic spiritual traditions. But, unfortunately, it's very difficult to describe in words a reality that is quite different from the usual rational level, often expressed through concepts and words.

That is why the Scriptures of the great spiritual traditions often use figurative and seemingly paradoxical expressions to point to it. Therefore, in order to access to this reality, the best thing to do is often turning on the intuitive faculty, which is closer to it than the reasoning faculty is.

For example, Zen uses the *koans*, which are paradoxical affirmations, as a means to help the disciples in transcending the normal level of rationality; their aim is to break the logical connections that characterize the rational mind, and this latter is actually an impediment to the comprehension of something that transcends the mind itself.

Of course, here we are not interested in treating or attempting to describe this reality, but only in outlining its existence. Its importance is essential for each of us, because it is the ultimate goal of our life; however, what I would like to highlight here is that in order to reach it we have to realize some stages of evolution. And trying to achieve those stages during our lifetime is of paramount importance.

The existence of stages of evolution has been proved everywhere and at all times by the life of many people. Those people have been unquestionably special, and life was for them a continuous discovery and an opportunity to express their potential to the fullest extent.

Undoubtedly, not all of us can attain those levels of achievement, but certainly each of us can make his own existence special, ensuring that it becomes interesting day by day.

No one is exempt from the effort to realize his own potential to the fullest extent. The world is full of people who practice the art at various levels, although very few become Michelangelo. But this does not prevent such persons to find their own way of expression. So it happens in the consciential growth.

To do this, neither enormous efforts nor amazing techniques are needed; it's all within our grasp. We should ultimately recognize what we already are; in fact, in our essence we are divine, even though we have an "ego", a personality, which is full of limits and in the ordinary level of existence is very far from that essence.

It's up to us making our existence special by going beyond ordinariness; in order to accomplish this, we "just" have to abandon ordinariness, just as if we left an old garment. All that is necessary is to give up our attachment to ordinariness.

The first step to make our existence special is *recognizing* that we have some limits. In fact, we must first know them, because often we never did. Therefore, we have a big work to do within ourselves, a discovery work that leads us to have a non theoretical, non mental, but emotionally felt knowledge of our inner world.

In order to move close to the core of our truth, above all we have to deal with things that are not working within us and in our life. There where something is not realized as it should be, or as we think it should be, maybe there is a limit that we don't accept. Often, what makes the things worse and makes us become stubborn and obtuse is the refusal to see that we have a certain limit. Then life becomes a real fight, which may prove itself to be also very exhausting in the long run.

First of all, we have an ontological limit, which is represented by the fact that we are not the rulers of our own life and we depend on

Another much higher than us. Can we accept this? If so, we will take our decisions and we will measure our successes and failures in compliance with this limit. Otherwise, we are doomed to develop anger and resentment towards a fate that we consider cruel. Nothing is more misleading, and responsible of early deaths, depressions, and premature wrinkles, than this misconception.

Beginning to recognize that our life comes from another source, which is higher than us, is a good starting point in the path of quest and of happiness. Those who argue with great boldness and confidence of being atheists don't really have any idea how much suffering are they inflicting on themselves, although apparently it doesn't seem to be so. Declaring one's own atheism doesn't mean only to refuse to belong to any religion, recognized or not, but it means – and this is even more hopeless – to think one's own life with no afterlife.

This kind of suffering is hidden behind an overdeveloped mind and relies on the alleged power of the mind itself, although it is disguised as a false modesty and as an open acceptance of the existence. Many manifest atheists intend this position as very brave, as true acceptance of the "reality" and harshness of the earthly existence.
From the point of view of the one who is open to a transcendent dimension, on the

31

opposite, this attitude may seem very babyish, insofar as it is very far from a truth which, albeit unproven nor scientifically demonstrable, unveils itself to the people who open themselves up to it with their mind and heart.

This is not the figment of the imagination of an excited or exalted mind: the divine essence within us, apart from intuited, can be even experienced. The great psychiatrist Carl Gustav Jung, questioned in an interview about whether he believed in God, replied smiling and without hesitation that he didn't need to believe, since he knew Him.

After recognizing that we have limits, we should engage daily not to forget it. It's true that we already make a great effort by agreeing to see them. In fact, seeing them in the inescapable events of life or simply in the feedbacks given by the same reality external to us, is often shocking in itself and sometimes we react dramatically.

However, in addition to accepting them, we should begin to love the very fact of having them. Shrugging one's shoulders, laughing at them, is not yet loving acceptance. This kind of love for our limits, apart from making us live happier, makes us feel more human and appreciate our human dimension, limited as it is.

In this way we get rid of many conflicts and we can appreciate our life passing, moment by moment. But unfortunately there are reasons why we can't do it, and simply wanting it is not enough. We often have to do a specific work of inner exploration, in order to seek out and overcome our defenses, that don't want those limits to be seen and then this prevents our growth.

A distinction should be made between the structural limits and the ones produced by ourselves. The first ones are related to the fact that we were born in a certain way, in a certain environment, with typical physiological parameters, with the physical and mental structure that we were given. And this has a profound meaning for our life experience, as the psychoanalyst Alfred Adler brilliantly showed in his studies on the organic inferiority in the child.

These limits are partly surmountable by learning to live with them, as many people can witness who were born in, or have subsequently acquired, a state of impairment, but later have transformed the course of their lives, bringing out unexpected energies and potentialities, apart from giving meaning to their impairment.

The limits produced by ourselves are all those mental constructions that we make as a result of the non-acceptance of our structural limits and also as a result of the process of idealization, started in early childhood but continuously operating within us, in consequence of which we expect more than what life can offer us. We cannot obtain this extra because we have structural limits and because our life contains within itself some innate seeds, whose expression doesn't depend solely on our will nor can be subject to our expectations.

Then, along with the work of acceptance of our structural limits we ought to do a further and bold work of recognition of the limits that we ourselves produce via idealization. This means working on our *narcissism*, namely, on the defense of our ideal image, that has replaced our true self.

In short, since we want more, firstly we build an ideal and in order to be up to it we form then an image of how we should be. Therefore, we forget about this unconscious process and we try to defend ourselves from any possible attack against this image of us, which we now believe to be real, while in reality it's completely fake. From here stems our mental suffering, such as panic attacks and phobias.

This work on oneself takes the space of a lifetime and can hardly be done by oneself, because nobody can work on his own resistances and idealizations as long as he is submerged in them up to the neck.

Anyone who wants to evolve beyond his self-produced limits must surrender to the idea of having to radically change direction in his life and undertake no matter what path of self-knowledge, provided that it is authentic. In psychological terms, this means doing a work on the shadow, on the parts of oneself that have been separated from consciousness and put in the repository of undesirable things, namely, in the shadow precisely.

In fact, once we decided, unconsciously, to create an ideal image of ourselves and then to be up to it, we highlighted what we consider successful aspects of us, while at the same time we cast many others of them away into the shadow. The shadow aspects are our limits, which we consider as impediments to our (assumed) realization.

However, only reading these lines or other more explanatory books is not enough for coming out of this mechanism; one has to have a melting pot where one's contents can be "melted" and purified.

This work is so important that we should all do it, even when we're convinced of going well, that is, it is actually a continuous work. However, it becomes indispensable when a psychopathology arises or, more generally, a block that prevents from living. Until this work is undertaken, we oblige us to carry the burden of our unconscious and repressed parts, which, however, do not remain silent, but are felt in ways that can be sometimes very bothersome and force us to stop.

Many so-called psychopathologies, first of all anxiety and panic attacks, happen often as a cry from these unconscious parts. Usually, people who suffer from them wish to put an end to these intolerable sufferings as soon as possible, with all possible means. And this is right and natural, of course.

But, if they don't reach the roots of their discomfort, after treating its symptoms, they haven't really solved the problem. The problem will inevitably recur at a later date, perhaps in other forms.

The shadow has been sometimes described as a sack that we carry back; the more contents it has, the more is heavy. The work we have to do is then to lighten the sack, although we cannot expect to be able to empty it completely.

Why is this work on the shadow so fundamental? Well, the fact is that by lightening the weight of the sack, all the energy that we used to drag the sack becomes available for other purposes. Exiting the metaphor, this means having the psychological energy to develop one's own potential, which before had been left in the shadow similarly. In fact, when we put some content in the shadow, we don't know whether it is really a limit or a potentiality.

Surely, when we repress something, we do it because we consider it as a limit, but later in life that which we have repressed could reveal itself as being a potential. Unfortunately, it is already in the "sack" of the shadow, then we forgot it and continue to ignore it, until we finally decide to begin emptying the sack.

One might underestimate the importance of this passage, maybe making excuses such as: "Don't exaggerate with psychology and all this work upon oneself. Basically, we are all limited; to be human means having defects. Too much investigation is useless, we cannot change anything of ourselves." This is a kind of depreciative thinking that leads only to the perpetuation of one's usual ways of being and behaving and, finally, to an evolutionary stasis.

The process of concealment that produces the shadow is continuous, out of our awareness and of the ability to control it, so it must be stopped as soon as possible and should be seen as a slow poisoning of the psyche, which gives rise to various kinds of suffering, with several degrees of severity. Then, why should we underestimate the importance of the psychological work?

Doing the work on the shadow or not doing it at all marks the difference between the chance of evolving and the certainty of standing still. Actually, there is a lot of difference between the two lifestyles: the first one is constructive and creative, the second one is boring and stagnant, let alone regressive. But, unfortunately, this latter is the most widespread and shared, so much that it seems to be the expected normality.

Now, the work on the shadow has various levels, because many are the levels of the unconscious. If it is done diligently and for a long time, it reveals little by little new and deeper aspects of self-knowledge. It is like descending into a deep well, with several "stations" inside.

A psychological work is not always a work on the shadow; very often it's not intended so much – especially by the client/patient – to self-knowledge but to relieving the symptoms of a discomfort; that is, ultimately it is conceived simply as a means for feeling better. This doesn't mean, however, that the request lying behind the symptom has been listened to; sometimes, it could even have been silenced.

Therefore, feeling better doesn't necessarily imply having done a work on the shadow, and working on the shadow does not just mean letting emotions emerge and reconnecting them to the bodily sensations. This work consists mainly in the integration of the shadow contents in the light of awareness, obviously as a result of a cognitive re-elaboration.

After having sensed and felt the unpleasant sensations and emotions related to the contact with a shadow content, the cognitive re-elaboration consists in understanding the experience at a rational level. It's only then that we can truly see our shadow contents, in order to be no longer dominated by them.

By working on the shadow we begin to understand in the "now" the relationship between what we think today and the mental contents generated in the "then" of the experience, that turned us away from those we have considered as undesirable parts of us.

Today almost all psychotherapies carry out this work, but their differences are manifested in their assumptions and, consequently, in the results that can be achieved in the long term as well as in the depth of healing and self-knowledge.

I personally agree with Wilber, the great American scholar and founder of Integral psychology (a branch of Transpersonal psychology), who states that every psychotherapy has its validity while at the same time it is more suited to certain types of diseases and developmental stages which the person who benefits of it inhabits. Therefore, each therapy can cure different symptoms, but with different methods and results.

Let us recall here that a person who suffers is not her symptoms, but she certainly inhabits a specific stage of development and, momentarily, has a symptom or a set of symptoms that she is unable to decode. Besides, every psychotherapy treats the symptoms depending on the depth of the assumptions from which it derives and on which it is based.

It's not by chance that the idea of psycotherapy as self-knowledge rather than just as the cure of a psychopathological disease is born within the humanistic context, the "third force" of psychology, and has become even broader in the transpersonal context, the "fourth" force of psychology (being Psychoanalysis and Behaviorism the first two forces).

Therefore, before undertaking a psychotherapy it's useful to take information on the assumptions of the approach followed by the therapist that is to be chosen, possibly reading some books on it. It is certainly true that the psychotherapeutic process is influenced more by the therapist than by the approach followed by him, but it is also true that "the apple doesn't fall far from the tree." Then, it matters a lot knowing what are the roots in which the psychotherapist bases his knowledge and skills.

Moreover, it's true that those who wish to grow not necessarily ought to turn to a psychotherapist, although it must be said that the figure that, in our current, highly complex and structured world, better embodies the role of the one who helps to grow in awareness is undoubtedly the psychotherapist. Once it was perhaps the priest, and perhaps it's no coincidence that today many religious are also specifically trained as psychotherapists and as such they practice this profession.

Therefore, the psychotherapist's membership in a scientific and institutional context, well defined and documented, is a guarantee and a protection for the person who decides to rely on him as an expert, for a period of time that can last – and rightly so – several years.

Ultimately, whatever the approach and the means that are adopted in the helping relationship, to face one's own limits is a delicate decision that requires careful consideration on the part of he who feels ready, because life calls him to do it, to begin the inner journey.

2
EXPERIENCING THE STATES
OF CONSCIOUSNESS

Among all the ways of being in the world, there is one that stands out from all others and consists in being present. This may sound like a vague concept, almost inflated for the frequency with which it is often cited in the literature of the self-knowledge guides (of which this book is an example), but unfortunately it's the only way to talk about something that is anything but a concept, being instead a way of being in the world, an attitude of consciousness that influences all of our thoughts and behaviors.

Being present could be defined as a state of the mind, in which we perceive reality with a particular quality, with a "light" that is different from the one that we are used to when we are immersed in ordinariness.

To those who practice meditation constantly this concept is familiar; it's enough for them to sit in the place where they meditate daily to attain instantly this state of mind. In the ordinary condition, instead, we are essentially involved in actions, feelings and behaviors of which we can be barely aware, even though they result from a project. We start setting a project and, in taking action, we lose touch with its motivations. We fall prey to the action and we detach from its causes. In so doing and in perpetuating this attitude throughout the day, for months and for years, eventually we lose touch with our own Self.

When we start to become more present, by contrast, we begin to use awareness in a way that helps us see our behaviors and feelings more objectively. We can therefore see them as if they were objects. We also start to reflect about why they have certain traits rather than others. Ultimately, we are more alert and attentive; so, we have a greater ability to see our mistakes, which we can correct for living better, with ourselves and with others.

This increase in awareness may be the natural result of our ability to process our experiences and of our inter- and intra-personal skills, but it can also result from a specific work done upon ourselves, that leads us to experience more expanded and comprehensive states of consciousness.

We can have a good ability to live consciously in the ordinary level of existence and we can, via a specific work, learn a new kind of awareness which leads us to go beyond the condition of ordinary awareness. This latter usually is aimed at the efficiency in the active life, but it doesn't help very much in getting in touch with the inner life and the deepest motivations.

The important thing I want to underline is that we can experience states of consciousness beyond the ordinary one, in which we are immersed normally in the waking condition. I am not referring to the altered states of consciousness, which personally I have never even experienced, that lead us undoubtedly to non-ordinary domains of the mind, but that, once vanished, don't necessarily make us stabilize in more advanced stages of consciousness.

Indeed, these altered states mostly end up with creating dissociative phenomena, because we are not able to integrate the emotions and impressions they convey and because, after having experienced them, we can find it difficult to accept the condition of our ordinary life.

So, why so many people are fascinated at such high a degree by the altered states of consciousness? Maybe, because they have a certain reluctance and difficulty in remaining in the body dimension. It's true that this dimension is a "heavy" experience, sometimes exhausting, but we cannot disregard it, at least as long as we are alive.

Thus, many prefer to evoke these altered states because they think in so doing they can overcome the body dimension, which they refuse. Then, when they inevitably come back to it, they risk to dissociate themselves from it. This doesn't pertain to the induction of altered states of consciousness in the context of a secure and guided spiritual growth, or as a part of clinical trials for therapeutic purposes.

Anyway, what matters the most is to provide quality and significance to the ordinary human dimension, provided that it is inhabited by awareness, this one not ordinary, of the existence of a higher dimension which transcends us and permeates us at the same time. Somehow, we all know this, but we have simply forgotten it during time.

So, ultimately we can learn to experience more advanced states of consciousness with the aim to integrate them into our daily experience, which is, and must always be, rooted in the body and in the emotions.

We should never separate ourselves from our body, putting as an excuse for instance the unavoidability of its finitude, then its apparent uselessness when compared with the spiritual dimension. I knew a young guy who died by hanging himself. In a farewell letter to the family, he had written that he wanted to experience the paradise that by her parents, fervent Catholics, had always been envisaged as a luminous reality.

Certainly it will be like that – all we hope so – but one has to be extremely separated from his body, being mentally disturbed at a severe degree, for committing such an aggressive act towards himself in that apparently dispassionate way.

We should apprehend how to integrate all of our experiences, both ordinary and extraordinary, in our current dimension, the one of a life incarnated in a body, with its peculiar difficulties and limitations. Looking for otherworldly or parapsychological experiences is totally useless for the sake of our growth. At the very least, it's useless if we are not able to integrate them, that is, to respond soundly to the question, "What does this experience teach me? What kind of changes does it bring concretely to my life today?"

An example of the extent to which some induced experiences can be misleading and regressive, for instance those induced by drugs, may be seen in analogy to what happens with traumas. They also imply the bursting in consciousness of unexpected and shocking elements. The effort required to process them is a measure of how much a sudden and amazing experience puts our system of values and certainties at stakes. So, that which is not ordinary should be integrated slowly within our consciousness, we need time to process and metabolize it. Sometimes it takes years, sometimes life itself is not enough.

Besides, if life itself sometimes sends us shocking events so that we understand the deep facts of our life, why should we go looking for traumatic experiences, and maybe even trigger them by means of doubtfully effective and useful techniques?

Certainly, we are given painful experiences so that we can evolve in consciousness, but this evolution should happen harmoniously and gradually, not in a carefree manner but by confronting boldly the challenges that life presents us, trying at the same time to feed the understanding of our incompleteness and the need to change profoundly certain interior attitudes we have.

Once understood this, we really start "running" in our life because we perceive that we have no time to waste anymore, and we don't do it in a compulsive way, dedicating ourselves as we did before to dispersive activities, but in the opposite we measure our energies and apply them in constructive activities.

Often we have an ideal of the way our life should be; there should be no painful experience. In short, it should be an easy and smooth life, the one we hope to live, the one continuously proposed by advertising.

So, often at the base of the search for altered states of consciousness there is the denial of pain, that we think we can overcome without really entering in its inside, by welcoming it. Actually, we tend to associate pain to sadness and depression. Instead, that's not so at all; depression almost always arises from the denial of the experience of pain, which is inherent to the human condition.

Earthly life is conceived in all the spiritual and religious paths as a means of purification and conversion and pain is, so to speak, the essence of our own finitude. Maybe, we may even stop to feel the pain if we could constantly live the experience of love, namely, acceptance and compassion.

Of course, we mustn't identify with the experience of pain nor we need to dispel it, by ignoring it. We have to feel it for what it is and whenever it manifests itself. Otherwise, we can become sad and, in the long run, we can weaken.

One particularly harmful thought, maybe also a result of a misunderstanding of the authentic spirituality, states that because the reality that we live is unreal, so is the pain we feel within us. Therefore, we might as well shelter in the pleasant but misleading altered states of consciousness, and open the doors of the "real" perception.

Conversely, as the great spiritual and religious traditions teach, most notably Christianity, the transformation of consciousness, leading to immortality, passes through understanding and accepting pain. This would be the descent into hell and, according to Christianity, the experience of the cross.

What, then, is a state of consciousness? We could start by saying that it is represented by a set of physiological and psychological parameters, by which we perceive a certain set of contents, of our reality and of the external one, in a certain way. A state of consciousness can be more or less widened, according to the understanding of reality we have.

The ordinary state of consciousness is the one in which most of us are usually when we perform the tasks of daily life, such as reading, driving, taking care of the household and the family, studying, seeing friends, reading novels, having fun, etc.

If we have for most of the time a state of consciousness, it means that we dwell in a certain stage of consciousness, manifesting itself in that state; that is, we think and perceive reality on the basis of the mental categories with which we are identified most of our time. So, our stage of consciousness corresponds to a stage of development, that is, to a certain level of consciousness maturation.

For example, the most common stage of consciousness, which for this reason we call *ordinary*, is the one that addresses the needs of adaptation. At this level, we think and feel according to the set of values that are required to be adapted to our society. This is normal and also right. In fact, if we cannot find a place in the space and time in we are living in, we won't be very adapted to life and probably we will run into hardships and difficulties, that can be often even very serious.

Adaptation to life was considered a goal for health from the first psychoanalysis, whose purpose was to enable people to work and to love; that is, ultimately, to satisfy the basic needs: essentially, survival, esteem and belonging. Therefore, reaching this stage in life is very important, otherwise we will have to struggle for living and being happy.

In the ordinary stage of consciousness we have a psychological attitude that makes us function quite in accord with the standards expected from our society and culture of reference. Usually, this corresponds to having a structure of personality that allows us to follow the rules provided by the society to which we belong, to make room for basic needs, to have more or less stable relationships, to know how to build and maintain durably some roles (work, family, etc.). This doesn't necessarily mean that we will be happy and satisfied, but at least that we will succeed in living a normal life.

Surely, if we rule out the possibility of becoming adapted, we will suffer a lot. For a teenager or a youngster, for example, to give up building an intimate bond is certainly more painful than trying it and having no success, as well as giving up fighting for achieving a social position.

In fact, those youngsters who renounce to toiling for the sake of building a position, perhaps because they are disheartened by a climate of pessimism about the future – only partly justified by the current economic and political hardship – definitely suffer from some sense of emptiness, which leads them inevitably to harmful compensations, and maybe drugs are not among the most serious ones.

Arguably, this introjected pessimism in some youngsters is at the heart of fundamentalist attitudes, outbreaks of xenophobic and racist mentality and violence upon the weakest. Obviously, it's not easy to prove the existence of this connection, but it is certain that all these behaviours occur in personalities whose emptiness has not been filled by more positive and lasting values.

We all have a varied amount of needs, which don't arise in the same way or at the same time or life stage in each of us. The great psychologist Abraham Maslow, one of the leading exponents of humanistic psychology and the pioneer of transpersonal psychology, described the main needs (or motivations) of the human being by placing them in a hierarchy, according to their power (pressure) and emergence throughout development.

At the base of the pyramid the security needs (physiological, survival) stand. Then, the affective and belongingness needs follow. Then, the need for esteem. All these are deficiency needs, meaning that they arise from the lack of something; therefore, they can only be satisfied by other people and in favourable situations. Then, the being needs follow, which relate to the realization of the inner potential, that which Maslow named *self-realization*.

Even higher in the hierarchy there is the need for transcendence. Maslow didn't describe it specifically as a need in its own right, but it was considered later by transpersonal psychology. The need for transcendence represents the tendency of personality to align itself to the Self, the spiritual essence of the individuality.

At some point, within the person can emerge a preponderant and urgent need for spirituality so that the other needs, maybe still present, are postponed or can even come into conflict with it.

The need for transcendence probably is always present in us, but there are special moments in our life in which the focus of our attention seems to be exclusively directed towards spirituality as a dimension to be investigated and developed. In these particular moments we can have real spiritual awakenings.

All needs can be present at every life stage, but certainly they are more likely to emerge in the hierarchical sequence described by Maslow. Moreover, they may arise, then return in the background and again become predominant in different periods of life, leading occasionally to inner conflicts.

Not to pay attention to them can often cause suffering, sometimes acute which, if not adequately treated, can become chronic, just as it happens with organic disorders.

Every need is inherently legitimate and it's only an unsolved psychological state that makes them appear in conflict one another. In general, there can be conflict among all needs, at every rung of the ladder.

For example, the need for esteem can go into competition with the need for affection. In fact, if one recognizes his own need for affection, one may feel less deserving of esteem, because maybe one doesn't accept the dependence status that the need for affection is believed to bring.

However, among all the possible conflicts the most important with respect to its consequences is the one that occurs between the safety needs and the self-realization one. The former are rooted in dependence, while the latter requires autonomy. In fact, the underlying conflict always occurs between dependence and autonomy, that is, between the fear of losing supports and safeties and the desire to grow and be creative.

Paying attention to a need after its emergence brings with itself a state of consciousness that can take many forms and manifest itself as a sense of fulfillment, a state of satisfaction and an almost undefined variety of emotional and sentimental states.

Ultimately, our way of being in the world is determined by our ability to respond to the needs, or motivations, of the moment. To dwell permanently in a way of being in the world becomes our current stage of consciousness. When we are present to ourselves, namely, when we know exactly how we feel and (partly) why we feel so, we dwell in a stage of consciousness in which the quality of attention begins to awaken. Of course, over time and by persevering in being present, we can also think about our needs and motivations and, if we wish, we can evolve towards higher needs.

Some may ask: "why do I need to evolve in my motivations? Life is already so difficult in itself: why complicate it even more?" The truth is that life in its ordinary dimension is terribly boring, whereas it starts to get very interesting as soon as our needs shift towards growth and being.

But, of course, as long as we live in a simply adapted way and don't seek higher motivations for our life, we are likely to measure happiness and well-being only in terms of possession of material goods or acquisitions in terms of prestige and esteem, that give us an illusory feeling of safety and stability. Instead, the state of being may seem to us rather poor, that is, devoid of wealth and interest, and sad.

Sometimes, unfortunately, only a depression or some serious traumas can awaken ourselves to the need to turn towards the highest needs and look at the deficient ones as fundamentally inconsistent. Who or what could convince us to abandon the safety, experienced and functioning, for choosing the uncertainty, the unknown, that additionally has no material consistency?

Actually, to take this decision is impossible if we have a mind immersed in ordinariness. Moreover, just only accepting rationally the idea of a radical upheaval of our motivational structure is not sufficient. We must start by implementing some tangible changes in our life.

We can easily fall into the consciential attitude of the rich in the parable, who moves away sad when Jesus tells him that if he wants to follow him he must give up its riches. Certainly, Jesus proposes a change in the rich's emotional attitude, and the riches represent the safeties that hold him clutched to the material level of consciousness.

We may think that we are happy with what we are and we don't want to feel stressed in trying to be something more or in yearning to a "being" that we don't perceive. In fact, put in these terms, relinquishing "having" for going towards being by imposition is very stressful. Besides, it doesn't even make sense to do it with such a state of mind.

Ordinariness may be something that we are at ease with. Of course, we shouldn't feel guilty about it, but we should understand that it's not our destiny and that it's definitely right to recommend to people who begin to feel discomfort with it, that they have to endeavour for overcoming it.

In this case it's necessary, therefore, to transform the mind, namely, to transform its usual ways of working, thinking and perceiving. Usually, the methods of care have this ability to transform. It's difficult, indeed, that in relationships, even in those where love and authenticity flow, that is, in the seemingly functioning ones, the desire of transformation leading to radically change one's own motivations starts up.

This book wishes to shed light on the difficulties that one may encounter in trying to overcome the deficiency motivations and to access and develop the being motivations, then dwelling in them and possibly giving them more and more space in one's life.

Since this is a really difficult path, that requires specific attention and a work aimed at overcoming resistances, there is nothing strange about the fact that it should be done in what I have previously referred to as a care context, namely, by means of a helping relationship led by experienced guides and well established paths, already experienced by people ahead in the knowledge of the structure of the mind.

I would like to point out that when I say mind I don't mean the brain, which is only its physical substrate, nor solely the rational mind, which is the expression of the mind in its ordinary state of consciousness.

We could say that the mind is the organ by which we perceive reality, both external and internal to us. It is inhabited by sensations, emotions, thoughts, but also by images, insights, and archetypal ideas. The latter were named transcendentals by the ancient Platonic tradition, and they are the universal qualities of the truth, the beauty and the goodness imprinted in individual souls.

Our mind, even though it has planted in itself the seeds of divinity, in its earthly dimension is limited not only because its contents are "volatile", impermanent, but mainly because it is identified with them. Then, we tend to take an idea, an image of ourselves, namely, an identity, and this is severely restricted, since it is linked to experiences of events subjectively interpreted.

The quality of our experiences has determined the construction of fences in the course of our development, which we decided not to overcome and that are also difficult to move, let alone to break down, even wanting to do it.

The structural limit of our mind consists in the fact that it has learned to function in a certain way and shows a resistance in trying to do it in other ways, namely, by using new categories and strategies. In a context of care – and the elective one is with no doubt psychotherapy – one works precisely for transforming the usual way in which the mind works.

The decision of working on it doesn't guarantee success in itself. Probably, most of the time one succeeds in accepting the nature of the mind but not in changing it. Changing the mind is a very hard task, and even only becoming aware of some facts that concern it represents a quantum leap in a person's life.

The work of transformation of oneself is difficult to be achieved in relational contexts. In psychotherapy, the relationship between the patient and the therapist aims at reflecting the facilitated person about the inconsistent operating modes of her mind, whereas the therapist is trained to withstand the projections of the patient, who defends himself in all the possible ways, often attacking, from those he perceives as threats to his integrity.

This distance between patient and therapist, a "therapeutic" distance that is also a closeness in itself, allows the facilitated person to objectify her own contents, disidentifying from them. This produces health and transformation.

In contrast, in an intimate relationship one partner hardly puts him/herself in the uncomfortable situation of mirroring the other one selflessly, so risking to be rejected or, even worse, abandoned. Yet, establishing such a link in an intimate relationship would be so valuable! I don't want to diminish the value of an intimate relationship at all. The only thing I want to stress is that this kind of relationship is not necessarily synonymous with growth of the individuals involved in it.

Apart from satisfying our need for affection, staying in a relationship should be of help also for evolving. And, if we are to evolve in the needs and move towards the being motivations, we ought to grow. Therefore, it is important to know the reasons that keep us tied to the deficiency needs and what prevents us from accessing the being needs.

If we don't evolve, we will leave the earthly dimension without having accomplished the essential task of our existence, namely, to grow for getting closer and closer to our deep Self, whose essence is spiritual. All authentic spiritual traditions state that this essence survives death, while ego perishes.

Whether we believe or not in a transcendent dimension, if we are honest with ourselves we can recognize that we feel within us a recall to universal values, such as justice, goodness, truth and beauty. None of us, even the worst person, lacks a yearning for perfection, the wish to bring to completion some projects that have a far-reaching extent than the ones associated with a pure self-interest. Let's go then to know more closely the conflict that prevents us from growing.

3
THE CONFLICT THAT
IMPEDES GROWTH

When we are hungry, cold, or we are missing something essential, vital, we cannot think of anything else: we need to eat, warm up ourselves, fill the void that prevents us from living, that makes us crazy. We can even commit rash acts and overlook our own despair. Such is the strength of the so-called deficiency needs.

Also the lack of a person without whom we don't seem to be able to live brings us back to that sense of emptiness and worthlessness, to the point that we can think we could not exist without her.

In such situations, our identity depends on the outside; "pieces" of us have been replaced by "pieces" taken from the outside. We feel we don't count anything without that person. And that is so, in fact. Since some of our pieces belong to her and since she is no longer there, also a part of us is gone.

If we look attentively, behind any mourning, in addition to the physiological displeasure for the lack, there is also a void because we feel we have lost some parts of us.

Often we cannot look and evaluate ourselves on our own. Then, in order to feel that we exist we may need to depend on someone else's judgment. Therefore, we may have an extreme need to be valued, to be recognized by someone who we elected as our reference model.

How poor is our existence, then! Given that that person doesn't look at us anymore, she does not consider us as she did before, we fall into despair. We literally feel missing the ground under our feet, we tremble, we feel faint. All these are somatisations that represent the feelings and emotions related to the sense of emptiness and despair caused by the lack of attention.

Of course, at some point in our life we can find ourself in a deficiency state for various reasons, but to feel diminished in our identity is another matter. If our identity is well established, there is no shortage that can ruin it.

We can suffer because of the limitations that naturally exist to the satisfaction of our needs and desires. However, if we are strongly convinced that ultimately we are not our needs, the momentary lack of something or the abandonment or failure on the part of someone don't prevent us from looking elsewhere for something more suitable for us at that moment.

If in a period of our life our basic needs are not sufficiently satisfied, for example, if we don't have the essential comforts, we can try to organize ourselves in order to overcome that hard time. But we can do this only if we are sufficiently self-confident so as not to fall into despair. To have a good self-confidence is necessary for cultivating the deficiency needs so as not to be deprived of whatever we need.

We should always be aware that we can at any time fall prey to deficiency needs. When they do appear, we must do our best to satisfy them, in the best possible way. At the same time, we should find the conditions for not being overwhelmed by them, that is, we should try to overcome them. Thus, we will be much freer internally. Otherwise, we will have to develop many strategies to avoid finding ourselves in a state of deficiency.

It is amazing how high the degree of conditioning to which we submit ourselves when, instead of overcoming the slavery of the deficiency needs, we get lost in a thousand artifices necessary so as we don't forgo them. Actually, only a work on awareness can help us unravel the mind games that keep us stuck in a state of dependence on them, that is, in a state of adaptation.

The history of mankind goes in the direction of overcoming the dependence on material bonds, to engage in more interesting tasks and activities. But are we sure that humanity so far has truly liberated itself from such a dependency, without creating other dependences, perhaps more evolved, but still dependences?

Actually, overcoming some material constraints doesn't mean overcoming the dependence on deficiency needs. Unfortunately, in enjoying a well-being state we cling more and more to material goods, and not only to them. We also cling to things that seem to have become certainties, such as a better health and a comfort before not even imaginable. Everything on which we are dependent becomes to all intents and purposes a deficiency need.

In order to truly get rid of deficiency needs one must overcome the state of consciousness severely limited by a restricted representation of oneself and of the surrounding reality. Therefore, only if one undertakes an inner work one can see, and then possibly overcome, the identifications that prevent from solving the dependence on these needs.

Simply put, if we are identified with an image of ourselves as needing nourishment from the outside, then we will really believe it and we will be led to try to supply ourselves with whatever we think we lack. In addition, the more we have the more we feel that something is lacking. All this happens, of course, beyond all our possible conscious control, that is, these processes are unconscious by definition.

Dependence on deficiency needs negatively influences our motivation for the openness towards others. Indeed, it's useless to think that we can give ourselves if we are still so dependent on external sources of nourishment in order to feel satisfied. Therefore, it's true that happiness means giving oneself, as it is stated by those who look from the perspective of the opening of the heart, but this becomes really impossible if we are not aware of our conditioning on our identifications.

Since it's free by definition, the act of donating oneself should arise spontaneously from an inner experience as a result of the transition to a higher state of consciousness. I don't mean, however, that this truth is absolute.

The desire to overcome the limited state of the ordinary mind can arise within us spontaneously, or because we are sorely disappointed and feel the inconsistency of our usual ways of functioning, or even because we are doing a specific work on awareness, or finally because of the coexistence of some or all of the preceeding factors.

At some point in our life we can be awakened to the desire to evolve and face radically the dependence on the deficiency needs. When that happens, a real revolution in ourselves, a real miracle happens. Then, as we give space to this desire, we start to experience some discomfort for our dependence, and to feel at the same time a great need for inner freedom. But this latter will still have to wait long to be fully felt.

At this early stage we have just a taste of it and what we feel most is instead the hassle and the frustration for not being able to overcome the dependence. Maybe, we fight with all our strength against ourselves to overcome the dependence and to access a new state, but we don't succeed, despite the enormous efforts made.

This discomfort is often the result of a mind that fails to understand the crucial passage that is to be made: we must first accept our state of conditioning, so as to surrender to the stream of transformation, navigating in it with confidence.

This is a very difficult and challenging endeavour, more than ever when the resistances to change are excessively strong. This step cannot be done if one doesn't work on the attachment to the ideal image of himself.

In practice, there seems to be a voice within ourselves (even while reading these considerations) that tells us: "Ok, it is true, one has to change internally in order to abandon the dependency on the deficiency needs. But does this concern me, right now?" In the end, we cannot believe the extent to which our psychic structure, so well constructed, that has been working well for years, should be shaken from its foundation.

It would be too painful, a real injury to the self-image. "It's impossible, definitely" – we think – "there must be another way." So, half reassured by this statement, we continue persisting in our established beliefs and go forward as always. Unfortunately, it takes a lot of courage and determination to question oneself.

But what is it that truly awakens within us when we decide to try to overcome the deficiency needs? And why living according to those needs makes us feel so limited? The awakening of which we can feel the pressure at some point in our life involves an inherent need to express our potential — something that we might be if only we wish and that we have never been able to be, because of the conditioning to adhere to conventional models and because over time we have built an ideal image of ourselves, cleaving to those models.

Maslow argued that if we give up being all that we may become (and each of us has his own specific "calling"), we will terribly suffer.

Seen in these terms, the expression of our potential is not an *extra*, that is, something optional, not necessary, but instead it is our duty. The failure to perform this duty is not without consequences, above all for us. Furthermore, this expression is not reserved for a few, the luckiest. It's a duty to everyone.

Realizing our potential doesn't mean that we have to produce something universally accepted. The potential must be realized because something higher than our small ego needs it. It is, in short, a real calling, no matter how one conceives it. If, then, this expressed potential will be also appreciated, it will be better for our ego, but in itself the appreciation doesn't count that much. Surely, it is gratifying but at the same time risky, if the ego takes possession of it.

In that case, the person proceeds towards an incomplete self-realization, in which the inner calling is somehow diverted from its inherent purposes, whereas the drive for success and recognition at all costs increases.

All that we can accomplish and that is the result of creativity is something that not only depends on us. Somehow, it derives from a collective heritage from which we draw and that, occasionally, with our efforts and skills, we can unearth. It is therefore something for which to be grateful and to be felt as belonging to us rather than something to be proud in vain.

Self-realization concerns everyone; not everybody, however, feels it as a duty and, among those who feel it as a duty, there are few that have the courage to face the difficulties involved in bringing it forward.

The evolutionary drive is present in everyone but not everybody applies it to better express their full potential. Usually, it is taken into consideration only for reaching the ordinary level of consciousness, which contemplates only (or nearly) the satisfaction of the deficiency needs.

Up to a certain age, to satisfy exclusively the deficiency needs is normal, because one must consolidate one's roles, gain a space in life, experiment and test one's skills.

On the other hand, it must be recognized that many youngsters and teenagers already have a strong drive towards self-realization and, in many cases, even towards transcendence. When this happens though, unfortunately, most of the time they are not understood or properly oriented so as to make room for these higher needs, without renouncing to conquer their own space in the world.

Living a life oriented uniquely towards the deficiency needs makes people suffer a lot. Much of the mental suffering stems from this, even though it may not be recognized immediately. Suffering comes from the fact that one's desire for acquisition and wellness is not readily gratified, and often meets the frustration. So, without noticing it, the persistence of the deficiency needs leads to the development of strategies aimed at ensuring affection, consideration, esteem and regards of various kinds.

He who has been clever in doing this during childhood will be then more advantaged in the rest of his life. He will be more successful than the less experienced, the ones that are called pejoratively "losers." But in reality both the successful person (in this sense) and the least capable are doomed to the same fate: run, run, run, whether one is a lion or a gazelle. This is a source of stress and emotional disorders.

Unlike the being needs, whose scope is potentially unlimited, the deficiency needs are limited by the fact that they depend on the environment external to the person. So, they totally depend on factors that are beyond the person's control. Much of the suffering in couples, families and other human groups lies in expectations that individuals have towards others.

There's nothing to do, it will always be so, until it comes to interactions where one expects something from another, be him an individual, a community or an institution. And one expects something from another because one feels somewhat deficient.

Conversely, the being needs are free and rooted on what the person already is in herself, without depending on the contribution of others; they concern cultivating qualities of being. Getting in contact with dimensions of one's being, before unknown to oneself, brings great joy, which is strongly connected to the pleasure of growing. This pleasure comes from the fact that when one grows up one leaves spontaneously some tricks of the mind, and often vices, that once seemed impossible to eradicate.

But why then, if the being needs are so important and their satisfaction brings so much joy, one clings to the deficiency needs? The reason lies into the fact that in order to appreciate the beauty of the being realm one has to have a particular taste and be able to recognize them as important, then nurture them.

Another reason, connected to the one just mentioned, is that in order to access the being needs a structure of personality is needed in which many conflicts have been resolved and is quite free from defenses, so that one has a freer relationship both with the internal and the external world.

Unfortunately, not always where there's a will there's a way. If we are too afraid, too much in need of consideration, if we have been too deprived in childhood, so much that we don't believe in our possibilities, we cannot open ourselves to growth. Simply, we will hardly believe that we can grow, no matter the good will we have of succeeding better in our roles.

Growing up means that we start doing what we really want and not what we think we have to wish, more or less in accordance with the expectations of those who have brought us up to our adulthood or of those who continue to do it. Simply, if we don't believe in ourselves we cannot get out of the preconceived schemes embedded in us, and we won't give room to our aspirations.

Sometimes we might even think that to follow our aspirations means to betray our duty and, basically, we will grant ourselves spaces of freedom that fall within the logic of duty: "I do what my inner authority dictates me." In any case, we will act without having truly internalized the meaning of that duty.

The shift from having only deficiency needs to perceiving the being needs requires a change of perception and motivation. It's something that looks like a route change and it is all interior, very difficult to be understood through ordinary categories, to which we are usually accustomed.

Actually, few of us have been brought up to believe that our life can change only if something changes internally. Usually, we have heard sentences like: "Get a good position, then you will see that your life will change." These sentences are partly true but they don't take into account the real change, which springs from our inside.

When we grow up we feel that all the collection of schemas and motivations taken up to that point are no longer adequate and we feel the need to become something else. The dress we are wearing is no longer fitting to us, it doesn't suit us anymore or it is worn-out. Therefore, it has to be changed.

Of course, there is a long way from the very first moment we perceive that and the possibility to effectively transform our life; maybe, this lasts long for someone. Unfortunately, the conflict between the safety needs and the being needs can never be completely solved. Sometimes, we have to be capable to live with it, even though we should never give up the fight for the knowledge of ourselves and of our aspirations. Firstly, we should know what our aspirations are.

In fact, we can unconsciously decide to detach ourselves completely from our aspirations or even ignore their existence. Then, if someone asks us what we want to do in life or what we aim at we can innocently declare that we don't know it, or that we have never thought about it.

Or, with a bit more awareness we can recognize that we don't have the ability and the forces to make room for them in our lives. Therefore, we have given up. Or, we can feel that our aspirations strongly press within us, we would like to make room for them but we cannot because we are afraid of not succeeding or that we can lose safety.

These fears are very different. The first one refers to the presence of an ideal; that is, we feel the aspiration but we have an ideal too high to reach, so we think we must do more than the requested. Therefore, in this case we may conflict with a part of us that requires us to be in a certain way and that judges us, making us feel not "ok" if we are not up to its expectations.

Conversely, the second fear is induced by a character within us who fears that in losing safety he could find himself in a state of despair. This character could be a child who feels very small in front of the world and who has not experienced the feeling of protection, for various reasons.

The fear of losing safety emerges very early in our life and can be determined by a real experience of insecurity and abandonment. With regard to this primal fear we don't know that the sense of abandonment and insecurity that we may feel now is very different from the one we possibly felt in our childhood, when our life was completely dependent on our primary reference figures.

What can happen to us today if we get rid of some apparent certainties? Wouldn't we feel a sense of great openness and expansion? Of course, to understand how tied we are to our tiny internal certainties and how this manifests itself in all of our parts, in all of our behaviors, in the quality of our thinking, we must have done a serious work on ourselves and we must have embraced our small fragile parts.

Personally, if I had never started this work I have no idea of the directions I could have taken and if I would have the clarity I have today about myself and the things I know about me, that still are a fraction of those which I suspect I might know.

Who knows, maybe I would have arrived to the same point by another way. But, anyway, it would have always been a way of knowledge, although different from psychotherapy and meditation. My luck has been to be able to take advantage of these two instruments synergetically.

At some point in my life I have agreed to undertake a path of truth, starting to make truth within myself and trying to overcome the resistances of the ego, which are many, ubiquitous and ever ready to resurface, especially when one thinks he has overcome them.

The path of self-knowledge has a peculiarity: if we have decided to undertake it, we can hardly go back; at most, we can take sometimes a break to reflect. But, once we have tasted it, and despite its many difficulties, it will be really hard to do without it.

As we have seen, the conflict that impedes growth takes place between the attachment to the safety needs and the desire of being, this latter consisting in wanting to develop qualities that are less coarse than the ordinary ones. The expression of our potential is prevented by not wanting (and not being able) to give up the secure base, something familiar that we have already experienced.

Of course, we have some resistance in making this waiver, since giving up requires abandoning our usual ways of thinking and our comforts, for undertaking an uncertain and seemingly tiring path.

To abandon our usual patterns also means having to change the image we have of ourselves. Generally, we prefer by far continuing to filter reality through the vision we have of ourselves and to measure it through our mental categories, often distorted. Behind our resistance there is an ideal picture of how we want to be or we think we are, and of course nothing is further from reality than this self-representation of ourselves.

Being the self-representation based on assumptions that we have made about who we are and on subjective extrapolations of the reality, there is nothing strange if all this results in a confused idea of ourselves (to a large extent we all are more or less in this condition.) Therefore, we will also have a fuzzy idea of the reality.

So, it is precisely because we don't have a thorough knowledge of ourselves that we tend to project our unconscious parts over the others. In addition, on some people we project some parts; on other people, other parts, and it won't be easy for us to understand the rules that we adopt in this mental operation, unless we do an accurate work on ourselves.

All this ensures that we can seem different to different people. Some will say about us, "He is a patient and empathetic person", whereas others might say "He doesn't listen to me and often gives curt answers." It may be that these two seemingly opposite statements correspond to two different types of interaction, in which we appear as different persons.

We are not two people, of course, but the different interactions seem to relate to two different people. Likely, this will be the result of differing projected images of ourselves, or projections from others, which are also discordant with one another. In any case, it's always a matter of projections, that is, ultimately, of unconscious, subjective interpretations of reality.

This consideration should lead us not to cling too much to our beliefs. In fact, it's highly likely that most of them are wrong. Actually, we can be anything and its opposite, as the studies on the personality by Carl Gustav Jung admirably proved.

The reason for this clutter lies within us. In fact, we are "inhabited" by different characters – our subpersonalities –, that are pieces (or parts) of us with their own independence of action within the psyche and with their own, peculiar emotions. They will make us act unwittingly and incoherently, till the moment at which, through an advanced work of self-observation, we finally learn to know and control them.

When we are not integer or, better said, integral, we can be caught by one among our many subpersonalities and act according to its constructions in different situations. Only doing a serious (and often long) work of exploration of the slums of our psyche we may, once we have become aware of them, prevent from acting recklessly our subpersonalities (that we will discover to be countless), then causing misunderstanding, incomprehension and a premature and painful breakup of meaningful relationships.

When we are unaware that we are caught by our subpersonalities, not only we give up the idea of having fruitful relationships, but we give up also the desire of developing our potential, that remains therefore untapped and forgotten.

Ideally, we should be aware of our reactions in all circumstances of our life, then we should avoid putting them in place, so as to be effective in our relationships, work, health, etc., and give space to our creativity, intelligence and will.

In practice, this awareness is acquired via an intense work, which also includes dealing with narcissism, the attachment to an ideal image of ourselves, which produces the conflict between idealization and devaluation. This conflict manifests itself outwardly in the confrontation with the authority and unfortunately undermines our relationship with the persons significant to us, our parents, the office manager, the psychotherapist, the spiritual guide, and even God.

Of course, the authority projected outwardly is the one that lies within us, but to see it and become aware of how often we project it outside takes a lot of work to be done on us.

The Asian spiritual tradition teaches that at the root of narcissism lie factors of ignorance, or ontological vices such as pride, greed, arrogance and personal importance. All of them originate in the strong attachment to life and in the fear of death.

Therefore, as long as we are in the body we must always deal with these aspects. However, if we become aware of them our life can really take another course, very different from the one in which we are unconsciously immersed in our daily life.

Becoming aware requires a continuous work on ourselves. Just to remember it or to have seen sometimes more clearly our narcissistic reactions is not sufficient. Our reactions will be back again and again, and perhaps they will be even more dramatic, because in the meantime we may have honed the ability to conceal our faults. Maybe, we will tell ourselves: "Ok, now I have overcome this reaction." So, the next time we will act it we will be even more disappointed with ourselves.

Indeed, overcoming our conflicts is not easy at all and requires patience, perseverance and tolerance of the frustrations. Therefore, since one has to start somehow, the solution to all this is, undoubtedly, getting on the wave.

4
GETTING ON THE WAVE

Getting on the wave is the only way to dispel our doubts and try to overcome our fears; essentially, it means getting involved, learning by doing. It is nice to admire an artwork, especially if it is beautiful. Even better is to try to create a work on one's own and realize how difficult is the process from the idea to its implementation. It is only putting oneself to the test that one can understand the process leading to the final, accomplished work.

The greatest work of art is undoubtedly to bring one's own potential to completion, namely, to make one's own life a work of art. It doesn't matter if there will be somebody that will admire it.

Surely, to do is better than not doing. But since here it is a question of embarking on a journey that requires relinquishing certainties, it's not easy to walk lightly on a path that doesn't promise anything certain but gives only some flashes of insight, at least at the beginning. Sometimes it doesn't even give any signal for a long time, and one can have the sensation of proceeding towards the darkness: "When will I see the light?" Actually, the light is there, albeit hidden from our view.

When a surfer succeeds in riding a wave, he doesn't know how it will end, he can fall inside of it, being overwhelmed and, if the wave is big, he can even die (of course, no surfer cultivates his passion having in mind the fatal event.)

When one goes on a trip with an unknown destination, the peculiar thing is that one can truly trust only on one's own intuition, which doesn't seem to be a sufficient motivation for proceeding. Yet, despite the journey – this kind of journey in particular – is risky, sometimes the alternative of remaining in the ordinariness appears far more unpleasant than venturing into an enterprise whose outcome is highly uncertain.

"Never leave the old road for a new one," goes the saying; and, in addition, those who have the courage to do it surely risk to lose precious time, should they want to go back to their old way of being. Maybe they have abandoned a lucrative job, or a sure career, or have given away the success in terms of a safe material consistency, or they have lost money in terms of missed earnings and have relinquished to the vicinity of loved ones.

When we decide to get on the wave, there may be within us a voice that whispers: "You are doing wrong," or "You have done all wrong." In the first case the voice can induce a strong fear, while in the second one a strong sense of guilt.

Of course, not for all people this passage is so conflictual, but it can take place instead in a harmonious and liberating way. For some, perhaps the majority, it can be very difficult and full of afterthoughts and indecisions, so as to arouse the thought: "But why would I do that?"

Certainly, much depends on the amount of conflicts within the personality. Yet, having conflicts doesn't mean that one should renounce to get on the wave. Solely, for such a person the path will be more difficult and hard and it will be highly suggested that he works upon himself to resolve them. The amount of conflicts resolved and the clear vision of one's own inner world will determine the ability to proceed quickly on the path towards autonomy and the being needs.

The more the willingness to work on oneself, especially on the parts one doesn't want to see or on the resistance to see them, the more one can get rid of the chains and constraints that prevent not only growth but also the perception of the need for growth. In fact, if the constraints are too many one cannot even notice the need to grow; at most, one can perceive an indefinite uneasiness.

This discomfort can be mild and manifest itself as an irritation, or become very strong and take the form of a maladjustment, not to be confused – of course – with the discomfort felt by him who suffers because he has never reached the basic levels of adaptation to life.

Not being able to make the distinction between the two conditions may lead some guides in the path of growth to consider an existential discomfort similar to an obsessive neurosis, for example. In the latter case, the personality traits linked to the controlling attitude are enabled because one fails to stop one's own drives; in the existential discomfort the same traits are enabled because one fails to direct the drives towards a creative purpose. How big is the difference between the two conditions!

In any case, the decision to get on the wave depends only partly on having or not conflicts or on having more or less resolved them. The discomfort one feels in denying growth is a signal that something must change in oneself, but the call to growth and realization of the being comes from the depths; it's a kind of interior "call."

So true that not all those who grow and go beyond the ordinary stage of development go through crises of awakening.

A crisis of awakening can be psychological or spiritual, as I described in my book (*Crescere senza invecchiare*, Persiani Editore, Bologna 2015), that is, it can be related to a need for transformation of the personality, which requires the growth of the ego, or to an instance that wishes to make room for transpersonal contents.

Sometimes these crises come together, sometimes they arise separately. Sometimes, the one follows the other. In any case, whether it manifests itself more on a psychological level or more on a spiritual one, the origin of our truest inspirations is always spiritual.

In the Vedānta (the last part of the Vedas, the sacred Hindu scriptures) it is assumed the existence of the Ātman (the transpersonal Self, according to the psychological view) and the Ahamkara (the ego, according to the psychological view), the latter being a reflection of the former, from which it is constantly influenced. Therefore, ultimately, everything concerning ego in its evolutionary aspects is inspired by a universal source, which transcends ego itself.

More simply said, getting on the wave, that is, trying to grow beyond the ordinary level, is a necessity that often comes from a strong appeal springing from the depths of our being and not always and uniquely from a selfish ambition, whose sole purpose is to unreasonably broaden ego.

The aspiration to grow is always positive but it's up to us to direct it towards a good expansion, that serves universal life and is not just a yearning of the expansionary and almighty ego, which in the long run proves to be sterile.

This is one reason why psychotherapy can be even harmful if it's simply aimed at expanding ego, and the expression of its powerful potential accordingly, without carefully dealing with the inquiry of the shadow contents, that can concern aspects of both the inferior unconscious (traditionally explored by psychoanalysis) and the superior one (taken into account by psychosynthesis.)

If we feel inspired to grow and we don't make any effort to realize it, or if, as stated by Maslow, we make a deliberate plan to be less than what we might become, then we will terribly suffer, because we have betrayed our deepest core, the Self. Obviously, it will be essentially an unaware renunciation, which doesn't mean that it will be less painful.

In short, we can suffer not only if we did wrong, but also – even though in a different way – if we failed to do good, that is, the right thing to do for us at that given time. In this last case we "committed a sin" for lack of awareness. That's why it's so important to develop awareness.

In the West we are accustomed to consider sin as a distance from God; thus, sin is the most serious fault we can commit. The feeling of guilt leads us to reparation and reconciliation to God.

Conversely, in the East the greatest human affliction is ignorance, meant as not knowing oneself, that is, the Self. It's the ontological unawareness. Restoring the mastery of consciousness, by cultivating attention, is one of the primary goals of our growth.

We should never look at unawareness in a tolerant way. Unawareness is the basis of many mistakes, and it shouldn't be justified only because we aren't used to working on it, and maybe we raise our shoulders and say: "This is a human limit, what can we do?"
The call to growth, although we don't feel it as such but only as an undefined discomfort, requires that we take a clear position: we should decide to follow it even though we are full of fears, or disregard it and postpone it to an undetermined date.

In the second case we may manifest our great unconscious fear. We don't feel ready to follow this call; therefore, our inner nature will knock on our door at a later date, and we hope then that we will be able to answer it.

Perceiving the states and processes I have described can be very difficult, also because we aren't used to talk about them with friends, confidants and partners. For example, if we go out in the evening with someone and try to debate these issues we can be judged boring and "heavy."

So, often we renounce sharing our feeling, because we don't want to risk appearing, or being, really boring. On the contrary, they are very important, absolutely not to be underestimated and to be shared with others, in order to grow together.

In general, although many people follow the call, not all among them get on the wave, because this means starting to transform their personality in the depths, agreeing to go to fathom, certainly with the due time and the appropriate means, the basics of the psyche.

Sometimes one can feel the need to change and grow, but has to wander indefinitely in search for suitable means, maybe even doing it all on one's own, however without being able to tackle the real obstacles, that are represented by narcissism.

The essence of narcissism consists in defending at all costs the ideal image we have built of ourselves. A part of us stands up as judge and claims to be superior to all, trying to kill in the bud all the attempts made from the outside to show us our limitations.

But how can we claim the right to be superior if in fact we are full of shortcomings and limitations? The destruction of all those who show us our limits is one of the characteristics of narcissism. Narcissism has so many psychological aspects and implications and so many are the clinical manifestations related to it that the purpose of treating them is outside this context.

I can only say that getting on the wave without taking into account one's own narcissism, that is, refusing to see it and, consequently, accepting to transform it, hurts a lot. And in the long run this is the main reason why we decide to "get off" the wave and to be happy with our supposed certainties. Consequently, we can even give up, temporarily or indefinitely, realizing our talents.

Maslow has taught us that we all have talents, namely, some qualities to be developed, and that we can be special also without being creative in a conventional sense, that is, being universally accepted.

In order to be creative – the great psychologist affirms – we should be like happy and confident kids, interested and focused in what we do at any given moment, without any mental superstructure.

Of course, if we have lived in childhood in a state of contentment, fullness and interest, it simply happened, out of our awareness. In our adulthood, especially if we carry on the weight of the wounds and disappointments and if we experienced failure in some way, it won't be easy to live those states spontaneously. Therefore, we must attain them doing a specific work.

Sooner or later in life we must leave the illusion that we can be happy and carefree as we were (maybe) in our childhood. To reach a state of balance and possibly happiness we have no other alternative than to go through a path of awareness. This is far from simple and devoid of obstacles, but it's hard precisely because it consists in coping with our resistances.

Resistances, as such, work against us without we noticing them. We built them so perfectly that we don't notice they are within us and we don't even know that we built them by ourselves. In fact, when we start working on them, we might have difficulties in accepting all this and continue thinking that they don't derive from us.

As far as we are concerned, in the depths of ourselves we think we have no defect, the fault lies in the others who don't understand us or, at most, it's all because of the unfair fate that occurred. "If only things had gone differently, today I wouldn't be the person I am and I wouldn't have these problems." How many times have we said this sentence, or we have thought it? And how little have we done so that things went differently?

Taking responsibility for our failures and omissions requires us to be able to recognize that we have long basked in the belief that the fault lay outside of us, because we never wanted to see honestly our perfectionism and our believing ourselves infallible, which made us stuck in a deadlock impeding us to become aware of actions that we ourselves have put in place and that resulted in failure.

Having this realization is no small thing and this is one of those harsh realizations that may lead us to the temptation to get off by the wave. If we have someone close to us who helps us to overcome this temptation, or if we are tired for having too often surrendered to these kinds of temptations and finally we have decided to change, we will continue following our path and growing.

In this case, we will no longer be the same as before. Otherwise, we'll take on again our usual patterns and add a new interior suffering to the one previously existing, arising from guilt for having surrendered.

Another strong temptation to get off by the wave is represented by the call of the people around us, who most often may be led to not understanding why we suddenly became weird and wonder what we are looking for and why we are not happy with our life, that appears flowing so harmoniously.

These people love us genuinely and certainly they stay close to us, but unfortunately it's difficult for us to explain to them, without them feeling rejected, that the kind of life we were leading before is no longer satisfying and that we aim at focusing on the being needs.

But is this love truly disinterested? Do they really care about our good, that is, what is good for us, or do they want to keep us tied to them in a selfish way, in the same way we were previously, to live together a common destiny of unawareness and ordinariness? Similar doubts come to light only when we finally decide to get on the wave and, from that height, we can see more clearly the inward chaos in which we were immersed.

At this point, if we are not yet rooted in our motivation to growth we may surrender to these calls, partly because we don't want to lose sure and consolidated emotional bonds and partly because we think that if we detach too much from them we can risk to remain alone in making an uncertain and arduous path.

In both cases, what binds us is always a need dictated by deficiency. These conflicts don't allow us to feel free. Simply put, we don't choose freely these relations on the basis of the need to share, but mainly to fulfill an affective deficiency.

So what are we really prone to renounce in the name of an inner realization? This latter corresponds to a state of consciousness and satisfaction far superior than the one resulting from having got certainties, whose function is essentially to fill gaps due to deficiencies.

Indeed, only if we can savor the light that comes from being we can take the leap and get on the wave. And it hasn't to be taken for granted that we succeed on the first try. In fact, getting on the wave is difficult if we never tried it before. This is the first time in our life when we consciously confront with a possible passage of stage of consciousness.

We had made some important steps, sometimes painful, like the one who ferried us from childhood to adolescence, but essentially we had endured them, we certainly hadn't chosen them.

We really have to dare for moving from the predominance of deficiency needs to the one of the being needs, because they belong to two disjointed worlds. Sometimes it's not even a matter of courage: we cannot do otherwise, we have no choice. If we don't listen to our inner nature – as Maslow stated – this one will press always sooner or later in order to be listened to.

We were born to evolve and, theoretically, our growth is potentially unlimited. The amazing thing is that, in theory, we don't have to do anything special, we "only" have to develop the ability to become something that we already are.

All spiritual traditions teach us that the path of evolution must be made within us, in order to discover something that we already are. However, we must not fall into the naïve temptation of thinking that this is easy in itself, by the mere fact that in being something that resides within us we already possess it. This is anything but so. It would be so if, at least, we didn't have a mental structure, a personality, an ego that thinks in terms of acquisitions and possessions.

It's the same naïve temptation that might lead us to believe that in order to evolve we just have to get rid of the ego. This is far from being so. Actually, we must first know it fully, then enter with it all in the spiritual domain. We must therefore develop a spiritual self freed from the burdens of the identifications, which compel it into ordinariness.

In fact, it's not that we don't want to abandon ordinariness, and along with it the dependence on the deficiency needs. The fact is that often we cannot do otherwise, although we would like to. Therefore, if we understand that we have structural limitations, due to the fact that we have a mind still cluttered by many conflicts, we must try by all possible means to resolve them. And, above all, we must develop the humility to allow us to be helped.

Getting on the wave, then, requires an act of courage and sometimes of cockiness, because the risk of failure is high and the guarantees of success are scarce. Somehow we feel that if we agree to move forward in a totally new path, so radically new, it will revolutionize our life and we are afraid that we will no longer be able to turn back or, in case we would do it, that we will no longer be the same.

In fact, it is so. Getting on the wave cannot be an experience among others: it's the experience, the mother of all experiences. It is a matter of deciding for the first time in our life to really risk, putting our life into play. Whether it is triggered from the outside, for example through a shock, or from within, the call to transformation is an awakening.

So why, if we wake up, should we then decide to fall asleep again? It can happen, of course, but if we have confidence in ourselves and in our intuition it won't be an event that will happen so easily.

How does a child, leaping from a small height, know that his dad won't withdraw the arms that must sustain him, in such case causing him to fall? He doesn't know, he is not even concerned with it, and trusts. In order to be able to get on the wave we should be able to be like that child.

Once up on the wave, then, we must learn to navigate at sight.

5
NAVIGATING AT SIGHT

In cultivating the being needs there is no certainty; therefore, one has to navigate at sight. Actually, certainties exist, of course, although they aren't the ones we are used to when we are predominantly dominated by deficiency needs. It's quite a matter of "uncertain certainty."

Certainty derives from a sentiment of safety, that can be perceived as something residing in the bottom of the heart, which refers to intuition, that is, to perceiving oneself as being clearly on the right track, the one indicated by our inner nature. Maslow speaks extensively about it.

This inner nature – as the great psychologist states – is weak, delicate and subtle, and habit, cultural pressure, incorrect attitudes towards it easily overpower it. But, even though it is weak, rarely it dissolves entirely, whether the person is normal or disturbed. Although denied, it always endures, hidden, and incessantly pushes for realization.

At this point in our path of growth we are firmly rooted in the aim to remain on the wave, nothing and nobody can make us withdraw, but we begin to be put to the test by countless difficulties. We can therefore be very vulnerable at certain moments.

The first difficulty is the doubt that continually meanders, even when apparently we seem confident of ourselves and of our motivations. The question that may arise in us at this point is: "Am I doing right?" It's a question that requires a corroboration, a certainty, in a path that is full of uncertainties, but that shouldn't contain any doubts. Who can give us answers about this dilemma and who can know us so thoroughly, but ourselves?

Surely, we can have someone reflecting us – and it's always good that we have some reference point, otherwise we can be self-deceived – but, in itself, the final decision on our lives is up to us. Hence, nothing can really dispel this doubt if not a belief lying within us, that can only mature over time.

It's a matter, then, of having the patience to wait and to cultivate the perseverance to keep going. "Sleep on it, to think about it" is perhaps the best suited saying to this moment of evolution, threatened by doubt. One needs to suspend judgment and make room for expectation, give oneself time to evaluate, without rushing.

Along with the difficulty of managing doubt comes the fear of isolation: "Should I do it all on my own?" Unfortunately, it is so. At most, in our riding the wave we can occasionally encounter someone who finds himself in our condition, who decided as we did to walk on the path toward authenticity and autonomy. However, he won't ever be a person against whom we lean, as it could happen once, when we lived immersed in the deficiency needs.

Anyway, probably we wouldn't even want it. In our internal code the idea of looking at others as safe supports is disappearing. Somehow, we realize that on our path we can ultimately rely solely on ourselves. This statement might seem an absolutism and indicate a pathological closure, but it's not so actually.

And that childish need for support we had when we were dominated by deficiency needs, typical of the child in front of the parent, we must learn to satisfy it within ourselves. Then, as it is sure that within us inhabits a child that never disappears in the life of the ego, it is also true that that inner child has a correspondent inner parent who can look after him.

By definition, the being needs imply the fact that one can tap only into one's own depth and not into another's one nor into the relationship, this latter becoming just a common place of communion. Its primary purpose is no longer emotional nourishment through dependence. For those who seek the being needs the only certainty lies in the evidence of being alive and of following the intent of realizing the being qualities.

It's not the presence of another that can fill one's own emptiness. The fundamental and basic need becomes now to express the potential that one possesses and the goal is no longer to be able to fill up a void, but to be able to pull out something from what before appeared to be a void.

In this regard, Maslow asserts that the self-realizing people – those who seek to satisfy the being needs – can even be annoyed by the presence of others, such great is their need to achieve the being qualities. This statement is so true that it is now accepted even in the collective imagination.

For example, in many sagas of fantasy literature, the hero of the moment, the one who has to carry out an important mission with a not egotistical purpose, it's almost always alone, though surrounded by fellow travellers. And, unlike the fictionalized stories, for example in many films, in which the central theme is almost always a love story, in the sagas the described path is an evolutionary process of a being who seeks realization. At most, the love stories involve secondary characters. So it is in the saga of *Star Wars* and in the trilogy of *The Lord of the Rings*.

Ultimately, the path of self-realization can be done in any personal condition. Thus, for example, both staying in a couple and being a single person. With this in mind, being single is not a depreciation, but it's even more desirable than the other condition. The need for self-realization might partially explain the increase in single-parent households and single people in the most developed countries. In fact, this phenomenon is not always attributable to an augmented individualism, as well as individualism doesn't necessarily mean selfishness.

A recent research, published in the British Journal of Psychology and led by Satoshi Kanazawa of the London School of Economics and by Norma Li of the Singapore Management University, showed that some people (the smartest ones, according to the scholars) wouldn't benefit from the relationship with others. Besides, spending time with friends might even lower their "level" of happiness. This assertion matches with Maslow's studies on self-realizing people. Could they be such "smart" people?

Our growth depends on the extent to which we can transform our habitual patterns of thinking and behavior. If we have stabilized ourselves on the wave this means that we are going to leave or overcome many of our defenses. If we want to express our potential, in fact, we have to be more authentic and then we have to revisit certain patterns that made us stiff as we are.

Simply put, those limits for which once we struggled in order to hide them to ourselves and to others, shall be used profitably for the sake of our evolution.

For example, a characteristic of shyness we had hidden because we thought, or we were taught, was something to be ashamed of, because it was considered synonymous with weakness, may reveal instead a great sensitivity. So, now we can use it to develop our talents in some field.

Or, if we have repressed some of our drives or particular ways of expression, because for whatever reason we had thought they weren't appropriate, we can revisit them, accept them and direct them towards creative goals. Or, we may decide to express them freely, but knowing the real consequences of their expression. But we must first overcome any possible feeling of guilt and shame associated with them.

In other cases, it could be a matter of overcoming the internal depreciative judgment that has always prevented us from asserting our own truth. In that case, we must learn to accept that we might be contradicted or disconfirmed.

As we can see, the difficulties related to the growth of a free ego and, consequently, the ability to remain on the wave, depend on the gradual abandonment of the predominance of the ideal image. Sometimes it is sufficient to feel, or even to wish, to abandon this predominance for feeling oneself freer, interested and open to life, resulting in an immediate releasing of creativity and a sense of a fuller life. From this follows a greater participation in daily life, that we learn to live as an opportunity for growing, to become more aware of our very essence.

Another difficulty on the path of growth is determined by tiredness. If fueled by doubt, this one can lead to depreciative considerations such as: "I may have it all wrong ..." This is a sign that we were expecting much more and that we aren't happy with accepting and working with the daily challenges as opportunities for our growth. This attitude is characterized by the difficulty to accept that our growth may be imperceptible, even though meaningful. We aren't able to see the small signs of change and we would expect impressive changes, both in ourselves and in the surrounding environment.

Riding the wave is somewhat uncomfortable, because there are no certainties in it and one has to navigate at sight. It will be then a matter of assuming a vision on life – this applies to every human being, from the least to the most fortunate – as an ocean of uncertainty.

Life is rooted in precariousness, but there are still some reference points, the first of which is its divine origin. The only real certainty can only come from there. And we need to make sure to seek this truth when we are in force and don't wait for the final stages of our life for starting doing it.

Tiredness is certainly to be avoided, it's not a natural condition but denotes lack of pace. We may be tired because we go through a period where we are living many stressful events. This can happen, but it cannot be the condition in which we dwell habitually.

If this happens, it means that we are doing something wrong and we aren't using properly our energetic resources, perhaps because we feel driven by an impulse to act excessively, or because we cannot say no to the many requests we receive from the outside.

There is a lot of work to be done to achieve a life condition favorable for our growth. Essentially, the first step consists – as claimed by all spiritual traditions – in purification, at all levels: physical, mental and spiritual. In practice, it is a matter of putting in place all the corrective actions that gradually lead us from a disordered life, full of harmful behaviors and ways of being, to a virtuous life.

If this path is rightly done, there is no obsession in it, one is no longer subject to attitudes of control – as can erroneously think those who confuse the sincere desire of growth with the constriction induced by a demanding superego – but one has an healthy inclination to order, both interior and exterior.

Certainly, it's not blindly adhering to a set of rules and moral laws, perceived as limitations on freedom and pleasure, but rather ascertaining that certain styles of life are best suited when one tries to satisfy mainly some deficiency needs – that leads to tiredness and a consequent need to rest and, very often, to laziness and untidiness – whereas when it comes to the being needs our energetic structure should allow us to be alert, vigilant and ready to seize any possible need for adaptation to the perspective of being.

Cultivating the being needs requires, like daily bread, awareness. Alcohol, drugs, lack of sleep and other countless habits and vices from which we are captured when we live an ordinary life, don't go along well with awareness; they rather contribute to blur it.

But it's not just bad eating habits nor unhealthy lifestyles that interfere with the being needs. Even thinking and our psychological defenses have their part in this self-limiting process. In fact, we must consider that anything we put into place on the physical and the exterior level has its origin in the mind, that is, the usual ways we think and organize our internal objects (sensations, emotions, thoughts.)

Therefore, if we want to remain on the wave, apart from navigating at sight we have to work hard on us, and assiduously, to transform ourselves progressively. But what is it that we need to transform? Essentially, our motives, what motivates us to act in life. Then, by directing the motivations towards being, also the needs will change accordingly. We will begin to think more frequently to what we aspire than to what we are lacking.

The transition from «to have» to «to be» can only be progressive and to remain on the wave means getting used to a new condition little by little. It cannot be achieved but in a gentle and progressive way. There will be no shock, but only a pleasant and gradual work upon oneself, although sometimes exhausting.

Besides, this work has unexpected consequences in practical terms. What we attain by purifying the vehicles (physical, mental and spiritual) in terms of personal fulfillment is far greater than what we could do even if we would hypothetically satisfy all of our deficiency needs.

But we must say that we may attach ourselves a lot to the being needs, although they are impalpable in comparison with the deficiency ones, that seem to be more "material." We may attach ourselves tremendously to the gratification of the being needs, and we can thus become very selfish and nourish the ego ever more, sometimes more than if we had fed ourselves only with relationships, esteem and other types of certainties. It is clear that, in this case, we are cultivating the being needs from the perspective of "having."

Perhaps, our true self can be attained only if we are willing to renounce daily to all of our certainties. Basically, we have no idea of that which life will present us each new day or if there will be a new day. Knowing this can help us to avoid attachment to anything. Ultimately, we can only be grateful for being alive and for being able to undertake a consciential growth, in case we aim at it.

The term "consciential growth" means here the tendency to be increasingly aware of something in ourselves that we didn't know before. However, often there may be the risk that we think we are growing, while actually we maintain our usual patterns of thinking and behavior. Our cosciential growth is put to the test in time and it should be supervised by someone who is more experienced than us.

Since the path to growth, that requires a radical transformation of the personality, is so difficult, it is important that we learn to use any clue or useful means in order to follow it constantly. We don't always have a clear idea of the fact that the danger of regression is right around the corner. Sometimes, it takes little to fall asleep and return to the patterns of thinking we have always had, and we hoped to have passed. All of a sudden we can realize that years have passed but we haven't really changed deep down.

Sometimes the latter sensation is only apparent and occurs when we feel discouraged because we don't seem to advance, or because we are assaulted by many doubts. In such moments, reading books on self-knowledge, self-development, can be of great help.

Sometimes, reading how others before us have tackled certain obstacles can reassure us and give us direction on how to proceed at best. Even the novels can be helpful, as long as they are not purely recreational readings, in which case they may be useful to relax but don't help us understanding how to grow.

Because when we are on the wave and we don't want (or we have no intention) to get off we begin to understand – or, better, we sense more easily – the consequences of our choices on our mental and physical energy level, we must take great care in managing our time and personal resources.

Usually, we start feeling that we have no more time to waste: we know that every thing useful keeps us going and every thing useless is likely to make us turn back or let us get stuck in our current stage, that we would like to overcome.

As we proceed on our path of growth, the circle of people with whom we can share something without being misunderstood usually gets thinner. In addition, since it's difficult even to us to understand what's happening to us, it's often best to be careful with what we share, even with the most trusted people of our circle.

In case we are having hard times in our consciential growth, if we are patient and can postpone, or at least reduce, our need to share, we can realize that our doubts and uncertainties will resolve quite spontaneously over time, simply by living the change. Of course, we must be able to accept the loneliness that this release brings with itself.

The best thing we can hope is that we have reference people that are ahead of us in the path, so that they can illuminate it, having already gone through certain experiences that we are about to going through. These people, if prepared and truly disinterested, can help us see those parts in us that interpose as obstacles to our self-realization.

Since in many cases these are parts that we don't want to see, it's not uncommon at some point that we reject the feedbacks that these people may give us and, as a consequence, we will risk self-deception and confusion. Many depressions at this stage of the consciential development may spring from similar dynamics, even in the most sincere seekers of the truth.

Therefore, if we want to navigate at sight and remain on the wave we must learn to manage wisely our relationships. We shouldn't use them to give vent to our complaints. Instead, we should take advantage of them for expressing ourselves in a free and open way.

If the person with whom we confront ourselves is more or less at our level, it will be very helpful to talk to her about that which we discover in us day after day. If, on the opposite, we have the opportunity to be in contact with a person who is more evolved than us, we should learn to listen the feedbacks she gives us with patience and humility.

It's very likely that, being ahead of us, she sees things that we cannot yet perceive. Normally, we cannot see ourselves objectively, otherwise we wouldn't be inconsistent in many of our expressions. So even a "peer" can certainly give us useful feedbacks. If we are sufficiently humble, we may accept them with patience and gratitude.

According to Carl Gustav Jung, we count for the essence that abides within us. If we don't realize that essence, we waste our life. Therefore, the realization of our potential is not only a means to fulfil our potential as an "Ego" in the world, and it's no option to make our life more interesting and fun. It's rather a moral and sacred duty, and we'd better start it as soon as possible, because it takes time, effort and dedication and, unfortunately, life is short and goes fast.

In order to awaken and understand what is the purpose we are born for, we cannot fail to activate within us the inner awakening that starts from the best expression of our ego. It's true that the ego is incomplete and closer to the material nature than to the spiritual one, but it's also the vehicle of the spirit in our earthly dimension. It is, in other words, spirit in action.

Therefore, we shouldn't separate ourselves from ego in an attempt to transcend it; instead, we must learn to distinguish the purely egoic motivations from the ones that come from our deepest essence. Both types of motivation manifest themselves in the ego.

If ego is cleansed of his narcissism, that is, if it's no longer attached to an ideal image of itself, it immediately turns in an incomparable and irreplaceable instrument for evolution. Therefore, navigating at sight means learning the precious art of equidistance, that coincides with the spiritual quality of humility: not being exalted for one's successes nor becoming discouraged for the difficulties, that sometimes are linked to an unaccomplished ego and sometimes constitute instead an unavoidable part of life.

6
EXPECTATIONS

We managed to get on the wave and we agreed to navigate at sight. Now, we have to deal with our expectations, which make up the shade of our path of growth. Actually, since jumping on the wave represents a significant promethean effort, there must necessarily be a counterweight that prevents from putting it in action.

Our shadows, always present in us (until we decide to shed light on them), are highlighted even further when we try to overcome some limits before never exceeded.

Like Luke Skywalker, the hero of the saga of *Star Wars*, we will be taken to deal with our *alter ego*, which experiences primary emotions such as anger and fear, and we would like to get rid of it, by killing him. And it is important that we have a guide who, like master Yoda of the saga, in front of our refusal to recognize that we feel such emotions reminds us: "You will feel them!"

The refusal to recognise that we have a substratum of anger, fear and pain, turns into expectations that things go according to our plans. This is a very important point, that sooner or later we will be led to understand, willy-nilly, while we are navigating at sight.

As can we easily verify in our own life, things hardly go according to our wishes. We can make plans – and this is good of course – but we should be willing to accept that there is an Engineer more important than us who often fixes them or forces us to rewrite them.

Of course, if we were willing to cooperate with Him, with an open heart, we would see beneficial corrections where before we saw only obstacles to our projects. But to understand this we have to make a step forward in our stage of consciousness. This truth cannot be understood by a mind exclusively based on rationality, no matter how advanced it is.

Actually, it's just the stubbornness of our ego that impedes the opening of consciousness. We can be unaware of this, even when we have started to be aware of a meaning of life that is larger than the ordinary one, that is, when we have already abandoned an extroverted way of life and we are engaged in a process of transformation. Namely, when we are firmly stabilized on the wave.

Unfortunately, it is precisely at this stage paradoxically that the main defenses of the ego are unleashed, which are perhaps the most entrenched and resistant. At this point, for example, if we have a guide that reflects and supervises us, we may be amazed of some of her feedbacks, that come to us precisely when things seem to proceed smoothly.

Conversely, maybe in that moment we are deceiving ourselves and our ego has put on a mask of he who is aware and apparently doesn't seem to have expectations anymore.
We may be shocked when we see dramatically that, on the contrary, we find ourselves in a defensive state, that manifests itself as confusion or even as a slight feeling of annoyance if not as a real aversion.

We don't want to abandon the hope that we may achieve our plans at all costs and the result, in front of a higher power that appears to frustrate us at every turn, is a subterranean anger, and sometimes not even too much subterranean. Of course, all these reactions can be observed and overcome more easily if we undertake a path of growth overseen by an experienced guide.

How should we behave if we are caught by these strong feelings? Definitely, the best thing to do, since we opted for awareness, is to turn our attention to them patiently, realizing that within us lives a rebellious child, who is never sated with pleasure. Or, we may find that our internal child just lacks a bit of attention. What does this more sensitive part of us really need? Do we know it, or do we continue to ignore her?

It is highly likely that we ignore her. In fact, even the spoiled kids have been usually ignored by those who looked after them, though apparently they were overfed and their wants and needs were listened to and satisfied in a timely manner.

The fact is that children don't have much need for affection in the form of excessive attention, but they need it as a help for knowing and managing their borders, on the basis of which they can regulate themselves. Very often behind our obstinacy in cultivating expectations there are similar dynamics of the inner child.

Surely, it is true that if we are at this point in our evolutionary path, that is, if we proceed speedy and with conviction towards the being needs, these feelings can disturb us, slowing down the path and making us feel sometimes discouraged, but surely they cannot make us desist from continuing nor they can make us go back.

If that happens, it means that we have proceeded up to the point where we are in a truly too idealistic way. We have to be very patient, because these feelings can come back again and again, until we alleviate or, even better, we resolve the conflicting issues of our inner child.

A great help in this comes to us from cultivating the spiritual qualities, most notably humility. The spiritual qualities can help us understand that, along with taking care of the inner child, we need to decrease the personal importance, which is the true creator of confusion and indecision to grow, and at the same time we need to abandon the identifications with conventional models.

Lacking qualities such as humility and patience, the ego is led to expand itself dramatically, putting on new masks, although more advanced than the ones it wore in a previous stage of development. These new devices of inauthenticity can lead to cynicism, towards oneself and towards others, and therefore to a probable psychological suffering.

We were born to evolve, but also to love. Probably, the main purpose of our existence is to develop the capacity to love. Psychology can point the way to love the inner child, that is, to pay loving attention to what happens internally. If we don't listen to the suffering of the child, we will be led easily to project outwardly our unresolved internal dynamics.

It's an almost alchemical process: by learning to love oneself in one's childish parts, many conflicts dissolve which are cause of incomprehension in relationships, of anger and irritation, dissatisfaction in life. The amazing thing is that this is a fluid process; as we take care of our inner child, little by little tensions are released. Even the mind becomes more lucid, the thinking process and the daytime seem to flow at a different pace. But this all obviously requires attention, failing which the process cannot be achieved.

The attentional process towards our inner reality shouldn't be taken for granted. It's not merely because he belongs to us that we love our inner child. Often it is true exactly the opposite, too often we neglect it, we ignore it, and only by doing a work on ourselves we can get to know the status of separateness that dwells within us. A part of us hates another one, which is always ours; she despises this other part and wants to get rid of her.

Working in psychotherapy the person learns to activate the internal dialogue between parts of hers that have stopped connecting one another, or that never did. The internal dialogue might seem a matter for schizophrenics. Indeed, people severely disturbed, namely, psychotic, express it explicitly, without inhibitions, being totally unaware of the process.

The majority of us, let's say, "healthy", on the other hand, expresses it in a less disorganized way but still unconsciously, by reproducing it outside symbolically, through behaviors and erroneous thoughts.

Therefore, it's necessary that we learn to recognize this dialogue and to understand it. In this way our internal parts, that before were disintegrated, by beginning to connect each other create integration within us.

When we learn to observe our internal dialogues, firstly for knowing them and then for healing them, we cannot do without splitting ourselves up into an observer and an observed one. One part of us gets observed and another observes. Via a relentless exercise another part emerges that seeks to mediate in a conscious manner among the various internal characters, who constantly speak within ourselves while we act, think, react and imagine.

This ability is considerably developed if we do a meditative work of self-observation, that reveals itself as being a valuable method of psychological self-knowledge.

The meditative self-observation, differently from the psychotherapeutic introspection, gives one the possibility to unravel one's ego defense mechanisms, manifesting themselves as particular reactions to particular situations. Their main function is to protect ego from those that are perceived as attacks to its integrity.

Essentially, ego fears its own disintegration and is alarmed when it perceives lack of safety. If we adhered to the being needs, meaning as we have seen that we have chosen them, it's common and normal that we go into crisis when our little ego puts into motion some defense mechanisms that aim at protecting its integrity, that is, its safety.

Thus, a part of us is willing to make a path of growth, agreeing to face risks, while another one feels overwhelmed and doesn't want at all to abandon the safe ground, super experimented and built over the years, from the very first moments of our life.

We oughtn't to become discouraged: this is our nature. The only thing we can do is to accept it and patiently try to transform this deeply-rooted structure. Patience is an essential virtue for those who want to proceed towards the needs of growth, but there are no handbooks to develop it. Often we learn it by dint of frustrations, that occur to us occasionally, when we need them.

Patience cannot be born in us if we aren't able to overcome somehow and even at a slight extent the frustration we feel for not seeing fulfilled our expectations. We should accept to take the poison of frustration in small doses, in order to fortify ourselves and to understand why we sense frustration and what it wants to teach us.

Indeed, frustration is somewhat an inevitable experience in life. It's up to us to accept it and let the patience take the place of anger. In some sense, patience originates from an inner voice that says something like: "Preserve your anger and turn it into an energy of tenacity, you will see that you will overcome all this and the next time you feel a frustration you will pass through it with the awareness of having more strength."

Just as one cannot suppress frustration, since it's present in the life of each of us, so unfortunately it's inconceivable not to have expectations anymore. What we need to learn is to have realistic expectations as much as possible, that is, the least idealistic and, above all, we need to be aware that we have expectations.

In fact, if we decide to relinquish them up entirely because we are afraid of having to experience the frustration, we can become cold and cynical. And, of course, we aren't called to this. It's better to be deluded, but having inside a blazing fire, than to have no desire, not because we are detached from it for having gone beyond it but because we have an extreme terror of being disappointed.

In order to develop and characterise within ourselves patience two resources are especially valuable: *time* and *silence*. They are necessary in order to enable *reflection*, without which one cannot develop patience.

Time is a vital resource. It's only by means of time that we can return calmly and reflectively on our burning issues. This is well known to him who is laboring at an artwork, like a sculpture or a painting.

One needs to return several times on the same piece and then leave it, because time creates a distance, a detachment from the object, that can then be viewed in a more calm, objective way. Features can emerge that were previously overlooked. Working artistically on oneself is like making a sculpture: only at the end of the process the work will unveil itself in all its parts, the way it had been conceived.

In this context, silence is the *conditio sine qua non*, the vital energy that allows transformation. Not only silence is important because it fosters concentration; it's also the creator of a suspension space, a timeless space, in which we can observe with more detachment both the things that happen to us and the way we are involved in them.

Of course, it must be first and foremost a silence of the mouth, namely, a wise use of the word. The next step will involve the silence of the mind, when the mind will be gradually pacified from the conflicts taking place within it, that produce mental chattering, where various contents overlap, resulting in a frenzied thinking activity.

Only then one can get to the silence of the heart, in which individuality, the ego, aligns to the Divine and moves back to let Him do the work of transformation.

We could say that to each of these three types of silence corresponds a specific degree of patience, resulting in different ways to go beyond expectations. To go beyond expectations is a synonym for a more harmonious and happy life. In any case, despite all the efforts we can make, we will never have the power to turn in our favour events that we consider unfavourable. It's far better to ally with life and abandon the idea of opposing to adversities.

When the superegoic grasp is loosened, that feeds expectations, everything seems to flow more slowly. The blocks of our existence are recomposed to form the figure of a jigsaw puzzle whose pieces we perceived before as apparently disconnected.

And, of course, if we have been able to get on the wave and to remain on it, because we have perceived and followed the voice of the interior *daimon*, we cannot really give up all the way we have done only because we feel persecuted by the fear that our expectations won't be fulfilled. What a great waste of energy it would be!

At some point, then, we can feel that we want to come to terms with fear. In that moment, perhaps, we may even perceive the urgent need to work on it, since it affects us so massively in the path of our growth.

We are full of fears, from the moment we are born until the moment we die. We fear dying first of all, but, paradoxically, we also fear to be born to a new life. As well as when we leave the womb we are shocked by experiencing the "birth trauma," in life we fear change, especially if it's a matter of a radical change.

Very often, unfortunately, life asks us to make changes that we don't want to make. Then, we try by all means to cling to the few certainties we have accumulated: a comfortable house, a good job, a family, some well-established relationships (all things that we have to try to acquire, otherwise we will be maladjusted.)

Even though we are probably among the most adaptable animals existing on the earth, it's really hard for us to abandon our acquired certainties, especially in times of materialism like those we are living, in which we don't tolerate that something doesn't go in the way we want.

Our times are dominated by the ego who aims at acquiring, and ego by definition resists with all means to whatever attempt made or perceived to lessen its sense of existing, that is rooted on safety.

However, we know that the sense of existing stems only partly from ego, but in reality it originates predominantly from that Essence to which we all pertain. The ego is just a "muscle," which certainly should be developed to make us adapt to the situations we encounter in life, but also to let us expand and embrace a wider sense of reality, in which to function better, with more creativity and satisfaction.

Finally, ego should align itself with that Essence in order to get inspirations and enter an existence with an even broader meaning, in which one can accomplish those superior needs that are considered as related to soul from all spiritual traditions. Therefore, if we are full of fears – and if we are honest with ourselves we cannot fail to recognise it – we don't have to pretend they don't exist.

We must not be afraid to be afraid, but we have to recognize it and at the same time make every possible effort not to remain identified with fear. We should be able to get to say to ourselves: "I fear, but I am not my fear."

Fear has an important role in creating our expectations and it is for escaping from the fear of fear that we create them: "Since I cannot tolerate to live constantly threatened by fears that crush me, I prefer to think that things will surely go well. My fears, no more existing, will cease to influence my life."

This denial ensures that we think things should definitely go as we expect. Expectations originate from this denial. However, since fear which is ignored continues to exist, the fear that expectations won't be realized will add to the fear of annihilation.

Expectations can greatly condition the course of our path of growth. It's for that that to manage them to keep them under control and possibly to overcome them is crucial for a seeker of the truth. Let's see now how this can be accomplished.

7
STRATEGIES FOR
NOT SUCCUMBING

One of the most difficult expectations to be overcome in our path of aware growth is the expectation that the path should always be full of interest, moments of joy and elation. Once we have experienced the joy of growing, because we have seen concretely the result of being interested – what being interested brings in terms of inner fullness –, we are led to believe that the path has to be always full of emotions and positive feelings.

All this doesn't reflect the truth. On the opposite, it often happens that, even though we are growing and doing well on our path, we experiment moments of boredom or times when we feel almost stationary. We are not stationary at all, of course, but we probably may seem so in comparison with our expectations. Our imagination gallops and creates illusions whereas we should perceive that the reality is quite different, anything but disappointing.

Boredom can be a humanly comprehensible feeling in the face of situations that seem not to change, both outside and inside of us, or that don't seem to do it as quickly as we would expect. Besides, boredom is not always synonymous with lack of enthusiasm. It can be both a resistance to accept that changes don't happen fast and a normal feeling in the face of the events. Also a part of our work can be naturally tedious, at times, especially if we can't really tolerate that there may be times when the activity flows more slowly.

Usually every work, even the most interesting and, of course, also the inner work, is made up both by moments of novelty, in which inspiration and instructions appear, and by moments in which a new project or a change has to be to put into practice, with all the difficulties involved in it.

However, this doesn't mean that the latter moments should be seen as boring. Simply, they don't always represent a novelty, but they are still interesting, because they guarantee the implementation of the project in view of a very definite end. The process of making is often longer than the one of conceiving, which preceded it.

In order to overcome these difficulties, we could consider our daytime as a sequence of different but not distracting activities, in order not to feel the hassle of holding inside the surplus of creativity that we seem not to be able to put in place constructively. On the other hand, if we have a lot of energy and creativity we absolutely have to find the way of expressing it.

Sometimes we may be led to believe that since we undertook a precise path of growth, the very fact of applying ourselves to it with all our heart, our mind and a well determined will, all this is a sufficient reason for which everything has to flow linearly.

In fact, a part of us tends to think that where there is a will there is a way and doesn't accept that, beyond all our efforts and our best intentions, things can go sometimes in a way quite different from the one we had foreshadowed. Sometimes they can go in an exactly opposite direction.

After publishing my first book (Nati per evolvere, ed. Psicologia, Roma 2012,) in which I had been engaged for three years of an intense study, I expected that it would have been very successful. This unfortunately didn't happen. Who was responsible of it? Was it the publishing house, which didn't facilitate the release and dissemination of a book by an unknown authors, or was it a fault of my expectations, that were too high? Probably, both factors have played their role. I want to exclude a third one, namely, that the book was not valid.

Anyway, a few months after the publication I entered a period of depression, seemingly unmotivated. Only after working on my mood, meditating and trying patiently to decipher its language, I came to the conclusion that it could be related to a matter of expectations. So, I was also able to see retrospectively how I had built gradually, in the three years of study necessary to write and then publish the book, an image of myself in line with the expectations related to the success of my work.

One strategy which can be very helpful for not succumbing to the frustrated expectations consists in thinking of oneself as being always a beginner, although one has being riding the wave already for some time. This mindset can be very healthy when one gets disappointed for some shattered expectations, provided that one adopts it with sincerity toward oneself.

In fact, it might be easier for a beginner to accept the defeat and work to improve in the things which he hasn't understood than for he who is already skilled in a particular area (even though sometimes the opposite is true).

To cultivate a beginner's attitude implies to feel strongly active within oneself the trait of curiosity and the love for the discovery and study of new topics. These trends can then be brought into one's path of growth, by conceiving it as a study of oneself.

Since we are for ourselves the most interesting topic by far, far more than any sophisticated philosophy, the corresponding study should be regarded as superior to any other type of study. In fact, it's a realizing study, in the sense that it aims at achieving new states of consciousness; therefore, it transforms us.

Whatever type of study certainly enriches us, broadens our knowledge and gives us new perspectives on reality, when it's not an end in itself, but not always it transforms us at a consciential level. That is, the knowledge resulting from a kind of study we undertake may be accretive but not realizing.

With the same curiosity with which one might approach the study of a new matter, in a new field, one should approach the study of oneself; studying oneself is like studying an individual who continually offers surprises. Naturally, one must have had in one's life the experience of having been interested in several topics passionately, or at least to only one but then having stretched one's view and having taken a look "at what is happening outside;"

otherwise, this kind of perspective is hardly feasible.

In the path of the aware growth what matters is shifting from theory to practice. Of course we need a theory, consolidated and tested through the reflections made over time. Even self-observation derived from meditation creates hypotheses on the basis of which we can try to direct our lives. However, until we decide to put them into practice, they remain abstract theory.

In moving to practice, we can see that some of our assumptions and considerations are valid, while others are not. Only with the proof of experience and time we can decide how many and which among them were correct and how many and which were simple projections, sheer consequences of our fears. In moving to practice, emotions and thoughts come out, reconnecting each other, often for the first time in life.

A further strategy not to succumb to frustrated expectations is amusement. Actually, we should learn to live our commitments, duties, interests, and even the path of our growth, in the same way as a happy and secure child would live them – as Maslow stated –, unaware of the "seriousness" of the issues of life.

Perhaps, too often we are conditioned by what we heard when we were kids, namely, that an adult must be serious. Therefore, at some point we are overwhelmed by seriousness and we give up playing, or we play in the wrong way; we fail to move from the childish game to the adult game, that is, we fail in making that the childish game evolves in a mature game.

This strategy is harder to be adopted than the previous one; in fact, it requires to have a good contact with one's own inner child. Otherwise, it's not feasible; that is, it cannot be adopted only by having goodwill, but it must result from a state of inner well-being, that cannot be present as long as one is encumbered by the conflicting issues of an unresolved ego, where there isn't still a sufficiently happy and safe inner child.

When one starts from a highly conflictual personal state, it can take many years of intense psychotherapeutic work to develop an inner tranquility, which gives rise to the possibility to adopt this strategy. However, knowing that a safe and happy inner child is the way for creativity and for lowering expectations in him who makes a path of growth and is already riding the wave, can be of help and open many scenarios, even different from psychotherapy.

In any case, it's useful to know that if we are not having fun somehow in evolving towards being, this means that we will fall much easier prey to expectations; to the extent that they are high, they will be regularly disappointed.

Having unrealistic expectations brings underground anger and a sense of helplessness. Anger results from the pain of deprivation deriving from the frustration of a need. When we expect something to happen that doesn't occur, there is always a need of some sort that is neglected. Instead, the sense of helplessness is associated with the harsh realization of how little power we have on events.

Yet, we have so many personal resources to draw from, if only we can accept that we are not omnipotent. To the extent that we can accept that not everything can go according to our plans, we acquire personal power; which is actually the real mental power.

A further strategy concerns the ability to let oneself go to events. This certainly mustn't be done passively, that is, by accepting everything that happens with the foolishness of him who thinks only to reap the fruit of life by believing that the important thing is having fun as much as possible. Being joyful and having fun is good, when one needs it and there is the possibility to realize it; doing it as a challenge and a remedy for not engaging in life leads to dissatisfaction and inauthenticity. Moreover, in this case having fun is not healthy and leads over time to a nihilistic vision of life and finally to psychological distress, depression and feelings of worthlessness.

Letting oneself go to events here means surrendering to the wisdom of life, or to the divine if we have a spiritual view of life or we are religious persons. After all, if we have got on the wave and we continue staying on it, this means that we somehow are willing to abandon the conventional certainties; therefore, deep within us we are already entrusting somehow to a higher wisdom, that doesn't come, as we know, from our small ego.

This ego, indeed, is not strong enough to navigate safely in the streams of uncertainty and precariousness; it rather tends to lean on material safeties. In the field of the subtle, towards which tends he who is evolving, the ego has little power of movement.

If we keep ourselves witty and with a playful character we find it easier to take things lightly, but we always have to take seriously the path that we have chosen to undertake. The path of the inner growth, in fact, is very serious; it's not a pastime.

If we have been riding the wave for a long time, it means that we are good observers of ourselves. We see what happens to us and we are used to the outbursts of our ego, who makes foolishness and creates expectations about how things should go, now that it is experiencing the elation due to new states of consciousness.

Even though we don't practice meditation yet, we already have a meditative attitude. We are used to believe that what happens to us is not accidental, such as our reactions to what happens to us. Everything has its place in the wonderful plane of existence and we are certainly part of it, but our ego gets excited when it sees that things are looking better and it tries to attribute to itself the merits.

In this state of affairs, in order not to fall victim of expectations, the exercises of disidentification by Assagioli may come to our aid. While observing a reaction or an expectation occurring to us, we can train ourselves to say: "I have an expectation, I have a reaction but I'm not that expectation, I'm not that reaction." With a constant practice we can recognize which interior characters are building that expectation and acting that reaction. And, little by little, we realize that we are not them.

Our life runs, so to speak, on two tracks: the first one is the life of the soul, the second one is the life of the ego. Usually, we follow little the first one; however, the few times we do it we are completely at ease. We are more used to follow the life of the ego, the one that refers to our daily actions, and that needs acquisitions and recognitions. The life of the soul doesn't take too much into account the thousand attractions of the ego and pushes us to purposeless actions, whose only aim is to express the qualities of truth, beauty and goodness, expressed in a thousand different ways and in different situations.

Our daily actions, our interests and passions can literally be transformed if we let ourselves be guided by the soul's will. Every action and field of our life can be illuminated by the soul's qualities, if only we give them space. This is the "magic" of the saints: everyything they touch turns into gold (in a spiritual sense, of course.)
However, we don't need to be saints for experiencing a bit of magic coming down on us when we perceive the soul, having given space to her. Unexplainable things happen to us and we can really begin to experience the lightness of living: everything flows better, without rushing (unless we want to rush), and everything starts to be more meaningful.

We can then begin to take on a lifestyle that is hardly understandable to those who live next to us. Often we are not capable either to explain some choices we make when we allow ourselves to be led by insights and inspirations. Of course, we must learn to discern which of these insights and inspirations come really from the soul and which of them derive from a construction made by our idealistic and omnipotent ego.

If we are truly driven by the soul's voice, there is no longer much rationality in the choices that we make and we must not ask ourselves many questions anymore; the important thing is that we live with confidence the diversions that the soul, if only we listen to her, provokes in the life of the ego, the ordinary life, full of worries, anxieties and hard work. We may continue to suffer and toil in the dimension of the ego, but with the awareness that we aren't only an ego.

Of course, to him who is aligned with the soul's will the frustrations of expectations weigh less because, in some sense, he has understood – or is starting to understand – that in the soul's language whatever happens, including the frustrations of expectations, has a profound evolutionary meaning.

It seems then that, in order to ride the wave for a long time, and possibly forever, until the end of one's life, it's necessary, or at least highly recommended, to embrace a spiritual vision of the existence and be convinced of the need for an inner path, which certainly is not without obstacles. In addition to the lights, there are many shadows to confront.

Therefore, the path of he who rides the wave must necessarily be directed towards the inner reality. The urge to travel, to see and learn about territories, landscapes and peoples, is replaced by a deep desire to travel inside. This also entails revisiting one's own motivations, traumas, past wounds, in order to turn them into an evolutionary perspective.

That which one day has limited us must constitute a resource for growing. In the end, what matters is not where we started from, but where we will arrive, mainly because once we become more evolved than the way we were before, we won't never go back again as before.

This must encourage us, because the purpose of our life is only partially acquisition; once we have got something, that becomes a certainty for us, we must evolve, we cannot keep dwelling in that certainty but we have to go further. Ultimately, as he who is firmly riding the wave well knows, the most important thing in life becomes to seriously undertake an authentic inner path.

8
THE LONELINESS OF THE PATH

Undertaking the path of interiority brings with itself an often unexpected guest: loneliness. Certainly this is not the sense of depressive emptiness that one feels when one experiences the lack of love or an existential crisis or when one is in the middle of a neurosis or another severe mental disorder.

In this case, on the opposite, the sense of emptiness derives rather from the realization that looking inside oneself in order to grow implies to find it difficult to share with somebody emotions and feelings coming from that which we meet continuously in exploring the depths of our psyche.

Maybe, for the first time in our life we truly realize that we are alone. The discovery of this loneliness can make us break down, especially if in the past we have experienced loneliness linked to relational difficulties or depression issues. But, in this case, we must realize that we have somehow evoked it. And this time, it certainly doesn't bring with itself the sense of void related to lack of affection, although we may live and colour this loneliness with feelings of the past.

At this stage of development it's almost normal that we feel lonely. In fact, who can understand our mental states, even variable, of surprise, astonishment, or sometimes of terror or despondency with which we come in contact if we seek some answers different from the conventional ones, to which we have been accustomed in the past? Maybe our past fellows, with whom we have shared the material life and have had fun? That's quite impossible. A new life has begun for us, and maybe it's time to look for new companions.

We may even realize, often unexpectedly, that we have little or nothing in common with our past fellows. This doesn't necessarily mean that we have to despise them or think that we are superior to them; it means instead that we are oriented toward different interests, so we can feel even a sense of strangeness towards the ones we were in the past (such as towards our friends of the past), maybe a past which is still not too far.

Ultimately, why in so many billions of people should we be so tied to those few ones that have accompanied us until then? It's more natural to open ourselves up and expand our influence and receptivity, establishing new bonds and letting go the old ones gratefully.

Should we be angry or disappointed because of this? Absolutely not. We just have to learn to accept it. The fact is that at some point in our life we woke up and felt the need to evolve. We couldn't avoid of having to pay a toll for that.

Later in life we will be able to understand how this unpleasant companion of our growth – loneliness – has been a resource, without which we wouldn't have perhaps the right concentration for following our path. We will also be able to understand the profound difference existing between loneliness and isolation: being alone doesn't mean being isolated; the opposite, instead, is true.

After all, it's quite natural to feel oneself alone while one is making a path that few can, or want, to do, even because it's not known nor it's considered possible. In fact, according to the collective imagination, growth ends normally at the very moment when the conventional roles (essentially, work and family) have been started and accomplished.

After having accomplished them (i.e., after putting on a family and consolidating a good job) one simply considers that one's life should continue horizontally, trying to gain more power and consolidate security, then waiting for the descent, to rest finally and get to the final goal, death.

Unfortunately, very few people can conceive their own life as a continually growing path, until the last moment of life, because they cannot separate the experience of the consciential growth – which is all interior and not depending on age nor on the roles taken – from the growth expressed outside, in the "real" life, which is essentially rooted in roles.

For those who have got on the wave, loneliness is both a curse and a blessing. It's a curse for the **part** of the ego that still needs certainties – including the affective ones – and feels annihilated by the fear of being secluded from a context, especially if one before lived a very extroverted life.

It's a blessing, instead, for that part which wants to evolve and really knows that in order to evolve one must silence the voices that would lead to abandon the enterprise. These voices instill the doubt, they invite to the sweetness of a safe haven and suggest that it's useless to hope for a different life – definitely, things will never change.

Undoubtedly, getting on the wave and remaining on it has in itself something truly heroic. One might wonder if one can live heroically starting from a personal state of mediocrity, or if it's necessary to be born gifted: who can respond to this dilemma? Nobody; just by getting oneself involved and trying, each one can find his own response. In my personal experience, I can say that it's worth to try.

Surely, looking at the example of the heroes of all times and places can inspire us, but it doesn't have much sense to try to follow in the footsteps of those who came before us and have had a universal success. We may risk of mimicking patterns of which we fail to be up. Can we be like Leonardo da Vinci? No. But perhaps not even he would have wanted to be so; he ended up being himself and before him the notion of being "Leonardo da Vinci" was unknown.

Making one's own life special trying to be the Leonardo that is within us is ok, it's feasible; rather, it's highly desirable. The geniuses like Leonardo did not act or conditioned their existence for the sake of being remembered, but because they couldn't nor wanted to be anything but themselves. And they succeeded, by expressing their talents to the fullest extent.

Who is too busy in expressing his creativity and in transforming himself has no time for thinking about being remembered or simply

147

appreciated. Therefore, we may find ourselves alone in a path that implies a deep transformation of our motivations and leads to an accurate knowledge of ourselves.

It would be very strange that we were truly understood all the way and appreciated by all people; it would mean that anyone understanding us has already done, or is doing, our own experiences. Since the number of people who evolve by "getting on the wave" is low (it has been estimated that only a very small percentage of the population of the United States dwell in stages of consciousness higher than the one of adaptation), loneliness is unfortunately a risk taken by anyone who ventures into new paths of awareness, and he who truly gets on the wave is in his own way a pioneer.

Maslow argued that the self-realizing people may feel downright annoyed by the presence of others, such strong is their need to focus on their own goals. In addition, loneliness is even unconsciously sought by him who does a path of transformation, since he is mentally too busy in solving problems related to growth, in observing himself while he acts, in finding solutions or simply in trying to give some answers to the questions that he relentlessly poses to himself in order to understand what is occurring within himself, or in reflecting on considerations that it's natural to do while things around and within him seem to change so radically and quickly.

And if it weren't enough the sense of frustrating for not being able to share with someone (and for those who are lucky, only with very few people) our progresses, the fact that the people around us may think that we are alone, that no one loves us anymore and that we are isolated – therefore we must suffer a lot –, increases the sense of annoyance. So, we are pitied; or, in the most favourable case, our near and dear ones begin to worry about us.

We can try to make them understand that we are not as alone as it seems but that we definitely seek loneliness more than ever, which means that we want to be silent, primarily. It's only being silent, in fact, that we can process the upsets, joys and interior surprises with which we get in touch while we experience new and more inclusive states of consciousness.

In addition to yearning for silence, we don't bear anymore wasting time in aimless activities. Of course, in this new perspective we are living even amusement is aimed at something. We are – or we should be – able to enjoy it when we need it, precisely because we recognized the need of it, but we no longer live in the constant need to "unplug", in an ongoing quest for relaxation and pleasant idleness, that is typical of the ordinary personality but on the contrary is absolutely stressful for those who ride the wave.

Therefore, we have said goodbye to parties stretching until dawn, comforting goods, mental numbness, long relaxing journeys, exhausting discussions and pleasant chats. Even our health will benefit of this.

Certainly, for him who has got on the wave and is unable to contain the atmosphere of pessimism surrounding him, in case his desire for loneliness is too evident, it's hard to manage such a climate, outside of – although not far from – himself.

So, at the beginning, whoever is on this path of transformation should be very patient, at least until the moment he succeeds in reestablishing a different connection with the outer world, like he is doing in relation to the inner one. By learning to be at ease in the second one, even the relation with the first one is readjusted, but it can take a long time.

Having withdrawn much of our interest from outer life in favor of the inner one, we have perhaps forgotten how we were once and sometimes we may have a devaluating judgement towards that part of us that we don't recognize anymore, the extroverted one. Therefore, directing our attention outwardly could seem to us a kind of regression.

If we can overcome this aversion for the "old" part of ourselves, we can look more indulgently at him who is still at an earlier stage of awareness, that is, he who is still strongly dominated by the deficiency needs.

However, even if we fear of not being understood, we must have the courage to talk about us and our changes, although not all people we knew before our changes can appreciate it. Many of them can, though, and far more than we might think. So, we can also figure out which of our relationships were authentic, if we were accepted for whom we were and who accepted us so.

This understanding can be very useful to us, because it gives us a clue on our state of identification with stereotyped models, that doesn't necessarily mean we can unravel and abandon just because we have got on the wave. The persistence in these identifications is very often an obstacle to the possibility of riding the wave.

In any case, we must not be afraid to leave behind people and situations with which we don't feel aligned anymore in our present condition. This is much more natural than we think; in maintaining at all costs some of our bonds, in fact, we merely postpone their ending; sooner or later we will have to leave them if we continue along our path of growth.

So, this loneliness of the path, which may sometimes seem like a nightmare, should be seen instead as golden, because it brings creativity. Not surprisingly the real artists, whose personal condition may resemble much to this riding the wave to which I refer here, crave loneliness and shun worldliness, because silence is fundamental to creativity; such as, therefore, loneliness that accompanies it.

However, it's not all that easy as it might seem at first glance. When we got on the wave, we somehow said no to our attachments, but we could fall into discouragement and feel alone as if we hadn't chosen this condition somehow deliberately, and we might not actually still be able to satisfy our needs when they appear. We may then go into conflict with the part of us that wishes to grow and feel even anger towards it ("But why did I put myself in this situation? Why do I do that? Wasn't I better off before?")

We could understand that we are not dominated by the deficiency needs, that we certainly need growth, but sometimes still need esteem, affection, material certainties. If we are not able to satisfy these deficiencies, we may feel as we felt before, when we weren't able to satisfy them. It seems that we are regressing ("But how, didn't I overcome these needs?"), we are assailed by doubts ("But, am I doing right?"), devaluation ("I got it all wrong"), confusion ("I don't understand anything, what am I doing?")

These moments can be awful and occasionally manifest themselves as mental disorders, such as depression, anxiety, states of exaltation or denial. Sometimes, it can be hard to make sense of them. We are temporarily confused about our motivations; maybe the path envisions to be very difficult, we are not yet ready to undertake it. Or, some of our unresolved nuclei have been awakened, on which we still have to work. Or we have fallen prey of idealization, and this took us to bite off more than we can chew.

Of course, only time can help us find the right answers and, of course, an experienced guide who knows how to steer us in the right direction. However, there are moods which are hardly expressible, even to a guide. She can point us the path and the most evident obstacles, though a large portion of our conflicts takes place internally. Therefore, only we can resolve with time our internal quarrels, by working intensely and using the tools that we are taught.

As we progress in our path of growth, we can familiarize with the idea that nothing in ourselves remains as it is forever, but can be transformed by means of a constant work on us. In short, our inner world is a forge and we are the craftsmen who mould and sketch the shape that we become little by little. Therefore, we shouldn't think that our destiny is so inescapable, but on the opposite that we may have an active part in it.

I believe that a high percentage of our future depends exclusively on ourselves and on how much we are willing to work to really change certain structures of thought. The main tool for doing this work of transformation is meditation and any meditative approach that works on awareness can be effective.

Whatever the path we choose for the sake of evolving and growing, it is important that in it there is no idealization and that we are willing to constantly test ourselves and to revise our ways of being and approaching our limitations.

If we tend to idealize, instead, we will also idealize our path of growth. In that case, we might perhaps feel superior to those from whom we could easily receive affection and esteem, and thus fall into crises dictated by deficiency needs.

In this case, loneliness becomes a condemnation rather than a condition consciously and serenely sought. The second possibility happens naturally and without traumas if we adhere in a really free manner to the path of growth. We no longer live conflicts, and an inner joy constantly dwells in us, for being on an interesting path, full of surprises and inner successes (unless we confuse these successes with the ones that our ego expects, i.e., continuous rewards and outer confirmations), curiosity and desire to grow.

Moreover, we experience the being in the present, so fears and anxieties of various kinds fade away. Life also flows more linearly and there is a greater creative and expressive capacity. We can experience, in short, some new states of consciousness and wholeness.

Maybe, sometimes these states may not be stable, but the experience of he who progresses along this path shows that they tend, over time and with practice, to stabilize themselves as stages of consciousness. Therefore, they ripen ways of being in the world that are increasingly more determined and constant.

9
WILL IT BE A NEUROSIS?

Among the fruitful encounters I have had so far in my life the one with Aldo Carotenuto has been undoubtedly one of the most meaningful. At the time of my university studies he was my professor of psychology of personality and individual differences. His lectures were very popular and incredibly intense on a very subtle level. He always managed to create an atmosphere of silence and interest, and this was not only because he was very well known.

Indeed, those few times that I happened to see him in some television broadcast, I didn't recognize him as the person who taught at the University. There he was the public figure; here, a great soul that had so much to transmit.

His lessons were held as follows: in the first hour he spoke about a topic for twenty minutes, then there was forty minutes interval; in the second hour he resumed the topic of the first part, going deep into it for twenty minutes. Finally, he invited to make questions.

We were a group of about ten students in following him even when he took part in meetings and presentations (he was invited pretty much everywhere.) So, one evening we were invited to dinner at his home. He lived in a very elegant apartment, with shelves full of books nearly everywhere, floor to ceiling.

That evening we "interviewed" him and he generously offered himself to answer our questions. He confided that he usually worked from seven in the morning to ten o'clock at night (he was also a writer and a psychoanalyst, as well as a professor at the University.) Asked why he worked so intensely, he frankly replied that the activities to which he devoted himself were all interesting. Therefore, he didn't need to rest, apart from the nocturnal sleep.

The only interests that diverted him from his study were watching movies and making occasional trips, which of course had always to have a cultural aspect. He told us that someone had suggested him that such a lifestyle couldn't be healthy at all, and he had answered him: "Will it be a neurosis? I don't give a damn!"

At that time I had no idea that the stages of development beyond the ordinary ego were clearly marked and characterized, nor I was able at all to distinguish the real authenticity from the indiscriminate expression of one's impulses. So, I was a little baffled at the idea that a professor of psychology of personality could be "neurotic."

Of course, there are different types of neuroses, and each level of development has its own neuroses. The simplest neurosis appears when we fail to reconcile our impulses with reality. Therefore, we must necessarily repress, or even remove, something.

In short, in order to be adapted to life and live a "normal" life, that is, in order to survive and have an adequate self-esteem, we must reconcile within ourselves the voices of duty, pleasure and reality. The basic neurosis prevents our way towards the adapted ego, and takes us towards a maladapted ego.

Only if the level of maladjustment is such that it prevents us from living and feeling rooted in reality, then we will suffer from various forms of psychopathology (which is dealt with by clinical psychology and psychotherapy). Otherwise, we'll be half-maladapted, namely, we will function better in some areas and worse in other ones.

To some extent, we all pretty much suffer from some form of maladjustment, or we have suffered once from it and now live with its consequences. I mean, to some extent we are all more or less "neurotic."

There are some areas within us that are not clear to ourselves – and of course it's good that we constantly seek to bring light on them – where we are weak, fragile, where our emotions are blocked or unrestrained, and where it's difficult for us to dig deep into. Maybe, we also have some problematic nuclei that we will never solve, because they are too tangled.

In riding the wave, the frustration resulting from this inability may make us feel very angry, and this usually corresponds to our idealization. In fact, in so far as we idealize, we won't tolerate to have cores of our personality that are still unresolved, or that perhaps will never be solved.

However, if we persist in riding the wave, little by little we will be able to acquire the aptitude to use our energy, that before we employed to hide these fragile nuclei (which we don't accept), for evolutionary purposes.

We can allow ourselves not to be ashamed of them anymore, and to no longer be afraid of being rejected because of them, so we can ensure that a space of creativity opens, where our tendency to control, our obsessiveness, will turn into desire for order for constructive purposes (we are no longer concerned about the horses escaping, but we want to open them the fence to get them to graze in peace), our fear of rejection becomes courage in the struggle to overcome difficulties, our uncontrolled anger transforms itself in an authentic and assertive expression of our ideas, thinking of ourselves becomes healthy selfishness, that is, the concentration on us to produce something useful even for someone else, the erotic impulse from an exclusively sexual impulse turns into creative energy.

But how is it interpreted, by those who knew us before our transformation, this change of course? I would say that sometimes it's not even perceived. Since it is seen by a less advanced level of consciousness, our new way of being can even be interpreted as a regression rather than a progression. We could easily be seen as contradictory, pathological, neurotic. Here is the truth contained in Carotenuto's statement.

Actually, it's not so; we were only more controlled before and we hadn't absolutely the courage to manifest our instinctual world, and in order to hide it we also concealed our inner wealth. Now we are learning to "play" with our contents and contradictions.

What's the difference between professor Carotenuto and a common obsessive-compulsive neurotic? This latter would spend hours and hours studying without knowing why he is doing it; the professor had exceptional time management capacity and creativity. He acted in the name of a *daimon*, a creative force that was calling him to devote himself to his task passionately, tirelessly; the neurotic instead is driven by an inner voice, of which he is not conscious, from which he cannot escape, and whose purposes are not creative, but on the contrary redundant and destructive.

Therefore, if we start to become creative, we may be seen as eccentric, neurotic. Of course, there's a long journey to become creative; in our being creative we can still carry with us neurotic nuclei, of which we are not aware and maybe we have never processed, and fall back into our old conflicting issues. However, the more we progress in our evolutionary path, the more we should be able to overcome our neuroses; provided that, obviously, we work hard on them.
If we have cores of obsessiveness, certainly our creativity will be influenced by them. Therefore, if we are riding the wave, we should try to understand what are they hiding. Otherwise, we will suffer unnecessarily and sometimes we could be led to accentuate our neurotic traits, instead of overcoming them.

The path of growth is nice but requires a lot of attention, because it can itself be inducer of disorders, that can be even serious. Sometimes we think that liberating energy is cathartic in itself; unfortunately, it's not at all so. To continue the metaphor of the horses, if we let them free we must ensure they have safe places where to graze. Otherwise, they may have to face many dangers, or may get lost.

Staying on the crest of a wave is exciting; so, if we are not balanced, that is, if we have not yet learned to control our impulses (better said, if we are still neurotic), our riding the wave will seem more as the flight of Icarus than as a pleasant surfing. Then, we may risk to experience many unpleasant things, such as depression or discouragement, that can lead us to give up our potential, consequently slowing our path towards the transpersonal.

In this regard, it's necessary to make a clarification about what is transpersonal and that which is spiritual. The term "transpersonal" refers essentially to states and stages of consciousness (respectively, temporary and stable over time) beyond the ordinary ego. This latter, as we have seen, acts in the world trying essentially to adapt itself to reality. With the term "spiritual" we refer to something that concerns a domain that is not closely related to the ego, although the ego takes part in it. That which is spiritual concerns a reality that transcends us and is not material in the proper sense; it's something superordinate to matter and to the world of the ego, and belongs to what Plato called as the world of ideas; or, in other words, the *soul*.

Being spiritual in a psychological sense also means being open to non-ordinary states of consciousness. Being religious instead is equivalent to joining an established religion and doesn't necessarily require to have a spiritual attitude (often the terms spirituality and religion are incorrectly overlapped).

Spirituality is a universal experience, which doesn't take account of dogmatic differences existing among the various religions and which refers to a common core everyone of them has. This core is the belief in the existence of a single Principle that rules the individual and the entire cosmos.

Now, we can be religious without being transpersonal, but we cannot be transpersonal without being spiritual. Transpersonal psychotherapy, with the integral approach by Ken Wilber, has as a specific mission the resolution of conflicts in the personality, that prevent the opening towards the transpersonal domain and any subsequent development of the spiritual qualities. Along with it, it aims at an integral care of the person and at her well-being, taking into account the four dimensions of being: physical, emotional, mental and spiritual.

In this context, it is crucial to develop a healthy personality, for which it is necessary to resolve the conflicts residing within it. A serious path of growth puts the person in front to her limits and to her tendency to reject and hide them. While our limitations are not a real problem for our growth, the tendency to reject them is a problem, and it's expressed as narcissism.

Narcissism refers to the attachment to an ideal self-image, so that one tries to appear better than what one believes to be, and it's a residual of the tendency, more or less normal in children and adolescents, to conceal parts of oneself that would prevent adaptation to life and society. However, if this attitude, that in the early stages of development is useful to growth, is not gradually abandoned, a totally unreal self image may be structured, with which it's very difficult to disidentify oneself.

Certainly this process of growth, with its challenges and obstacles, is more successful if it is accompanied by humility and, in general, by spiritual qualities, such as patience, harmony, confidence, etc. Therefore, cultivating a healthy spirituality, allied with a psychological work of transformation of one's own unsolved nuclei, is of paramount importance.

10
CULTIVATING A
HEALTHY SPIRITUALITY

Since we decided to grow and we weren't happy with adhering to established patterns of life, so much experimented and conventional, we have necessarily followed an inner recall that invites us to overcome the limited constraints of the ego.

This appeal, that we committed to follow apparently risking every precious thing we possess in life – the certainties, in their various forms –, is too strong for coming from that part of us that once adhered to common, conventional values. Where does it come from then? Certainly, it comes from a part of us that is truer, more authentic, and that we are slowly beginning to listen and appreciate.

But why has this voice become apparent suddenly, at a time when we maybe seem to be in balance? Perhaps, it means that that part was already there, but it was only sleeping and something has intervened in awaking it: who did that?

A part of us needed to be awakened, we don't know why; sooner or later we might realize that life is made up of awakenings, whether we like it or not. We can resist them, but certainly we cannot prevent our inner nature from making efforts to ensure that we pay attention to them. Of course, to our ego this is not okay, because this obliges it to question itself, to slow down or deviate from its roadmap.

Once we have acknowledged that we have an inner nature, a *deus ex machina* who speaks within us and sometimes suggests something, to recognize a spiritual dimension of life, something that stands above us completely, it's an almost consequent step.

In this acknowledgement there is nothing rational, of course. In fact, the rational mind doesn't admit the existence of an inner nature. But when this latter lets itself feel and we accept to listen to it, we are activating the spiritual intelligence within us, the faculty which is present in all of us – to varying degrees – and which makes us tune in to the higher things, just as the emotional intelligence allows us to read our emotions and those of other people.

Maslow studied the *peak experiences*, in which the personality is flooded with extraordinary contents, inspirations and insights beyond the domain of the ordinary experience. Since they are enlightened states, that bring joy and intense emotions and openness to the Absolute, it's impossible to ignore them when they occur in our lives. They are clearly too amazing to be catalogued as simple altered states in an ill consciousness.

Therefore, those who experience them are rarely prone to ignore them, even though they may not want to share them with anyone for fear of being misunderstood. Often the peak experiences become pivotal experiences in a person's life, both because they can reveal themselves as highly transformative and because their memory is indelible and generates deep meanings for that person.

Then, it's almost consequential that he who got on the wave, and is riding it, may experience that the boost to growth comes from a spiritual domain; so, he most likely will try to cultivate spirituality as a dimension of life deeply engaging and not as an experience among the many he could have. It becomes progressively the substrate of all the other activities and turns out to be the most indispensable thing in one's life. Anyway, this firmness strenghtens itself little by little and is a result of a gradual and natural transformation of one's motivations.

Transpersonal psychology, especially in its integral approach, which has Laura Boggio Gilot as the most prominent italian exponent, works to get this metanoia of personality, in which spirituality enters fully. It tries to start progressively the metamorphosis of personality, without creating traumas or breaks with the ego; indeed, it facilitates ego integration, in order to align it to the spiritual needs.

So, he who rides the wave will in all probability commit himself to a serious path of exploration of the spiritual dimension; for instance, by practicing meditation or going deep into the path of religious faith, or both. Willy-nilly, he who is on the wave starts to vibrate with spiritual energy, something that wasn't there before and now illuminates his life, guiding it by means of a new awareness. This latter is expressed as the quality of a more synthetic mind, which knows how to better seize the links between the occurring events, trying to discover meanings never perceived up to that moment.

It may happen that the person experiences for the first time authenticity in her life, the brilliance of this experience, and begins to do things that before she judged insignificant; she begins to take into consideration the "things of the spirit" as real as, if not more than, the "real" ones.

It's an important passage between stages of consciousness, a real upheaval in one's own interior life and perception.

Everything changes and takes on a much broader perspective. Everything acquires more color, interest, meaning. Experiences such as depression become a vague memory; or, if they occur again, they can be more easily overcome through the awareness of one's own inner dialogues, which take place among characters that are now better recognizable.

What happens when we embrace a spiritual vision by assimilating it in applying it in our everyday life? It happens that we begin to grow at last and we begin to do it by contracting instead of expanding ourselves. To be more precise, it's now a matter of expanding towards the interior, along with the possibility to experience an evolution beyond the ordinary stage of consciousness. The growth in this sense becomes an inner experience, that is often hardly communicable.

Being accustomed to think that growth consists of material, clearly visible, expressions we can hardly understand the signals of a genuine inner growth. To untrained eyes, indeed, he who grows internally may appear motionless, sometimes boring, or even weird; an almost suspicious person, closed in her world. Therefore, a person to beware of or not too much trustworthy.

Moreover, a person who grows tends to stop hiding herself behind her masks; so, for untrained eyes, the contradictions that unavoidably emerge when one is more authentic appear as symptoms of eccentricity and unreliability.

In growth, contraction is a natural evolution of expansion. In fact, it's the ego that expands itself but, after doing that and having expressed itself at its highest levels, so that it is fully satisfied, it will have to turn to the Self, that is, it will have to expand itself in consciousness by developing spiritual qualities.

Some of these qualities, that are traditionally taken into consideration by poetry and literature, are actually still part of the domain of the expansive ego, that expands itself in this case in less material areas of life, but still not spiritual in the proper sense. For example, sensitivity, sweetness are subtler qualities than the ordinary ones, but in itself they are not strictly spiritual.

The true spiritual qualities can be developed only when the ego starts to follow the will of the Self. In practice, this happens when one starts accepting that one's own life has a meaning only if it's addressed and dedicated to meeting the needs of the soul. Then, one can start to realize what he was born for, what truly matters to oneself in the long journey of the "return to the Father."

Probably, when we get on the wave, hoping then to remain there and continue the path on its crest, we don't know what direction we will take in our life, and maybe we will never thoroughly understand what will be our destiny and why do we have to go through so many trials.

We decided to undertake a risky path because we heard within us a strong call, but it will take us perhaps a long time to decipher the meaning of this call, that is however so strong as to test the certainties of the ego, on which often are based all our certainties and, ultimately, our same certainty to exist.

Only those who have done this passage can understand how strong the attachment to one's own certainties is. If we persist in this attachment, we can be children never grown up till the end of our existence.

Maybe, we could also be very adapted and we may have developed over time very solid supports: a solid career, a large family, a wide circle of friends, a nice house, we could be estimated as professionals, artists, or simply as persons.

But when some of these certainties fail, or just stagger a bit, not only we sense a normal mourning for the loss and the rejection of suffering, but the very foundations of our being are shooked. Then, the normal sadness of grief turns into depression because we no longer recognize ourselves: "But then, who am I now?"

At the roots of many existential depressions there is a similar dynamic.

The push to growth is an intrinsic property of the ego, that certainly has to be cultivated. However, it cannot take place without a call of a different nature. All traditions assert that life continues after death. So, if we die it means that the ego dies but another part survives. Therefore, ego is not the most important part of our identity.

As a consequence, no matter if it won't express itself fully in our life. Of course, we have to try to encourage its expression, not only because it brings health, but because the ultimate goal is to free it from its conflicts and then open it up to the Self.

This means in practice that if we want to make sense of our riding the wave, we must sooner or later undertake a path of spiritual evolution, and this evolution cannot happen if the ego is too conflictual. That's why, whether the ego expresses itself at its highest levels or not, in any case it must be healed in every possible way. Otherwise, its unresolved conflicts will affect the spiritual motivations, making them inconsistent and inauthentic, or – which is even worse – they will create new conflicts.

Ultimately, in speaking of growth we somewhat imply spirituality. We can say that, at whatever level our growth takes place, behind it there is some spiritual strength and inspiration.

Of course, a mature and healing spirituality cannot be but transforming. It "does not seek emotions and consolations, nor mystical experiences, but refers to a meditative discipline of study and inner practices that enter deeply into the life of the meditator and that has a purpose of transformation aimed at developing spiritual qualities and dissolving illusions and factors of suffering that separate the ego from its Essence and paralyze the path of development. This spirituality is functional to the integral knowledge of oneself and to the discovering of the meaning and task of life, as well as the development of maturity and wisdom" (from the interview to Laura Boggio Gilot, "Spirituality that transforms", www.aipt.it).

Cultivating a healthy spirituality implies, then, adhering to a project of slow and patient transformation, based on a discipline that is also a reeducation to the deepest, eternal values, forgotten or overlooked with the expansive process of the ego, which has made us get away from our Essence.

A healing spirituality brings, as well as maturity and wisdom, the opening of the heart, love, a fundamental element for the acceptance of one's own limits and flaws and, ultimately, for our own growth.

11
LOVING FOR GROWING

Ultimately, in order to grow healthy and strong, we need to love. We may also want loneliness and get out extraversion – this helps us grow in consciousness – but we cannot do without love.

We shouldn't confuse the need for self-realization, autonomy and creativity, with self-sufficiency, that is, being sufficient to ourselves for being happy. We need to love, at whichever level we are in our path of consciousness evolution.

Certainly, if we are self-realizing, we will begin to love without feeling the dependence on the other; we will no longer fear loving nor being abandoned, because we experience love as a wonderful and irreplaceable opportunity for exchange and mutual nourishment.

We often have to learn or re-learn to love, because maybe nobody taught us to love when we were kids, or we have forgotten it over time, hardening our heart in the belief that to develop and assert ourselves we couldn't devote our time to listen to our feelings.

We may have made confusion between childhood and sentiment, mistakenly thinking that having passed the former meant similarly sacrificing the latter.

To love means leaving the door of the heart open, trusting that an influence of goodness and fullness can descend from above, meaning that we can live and act lightly, knowing that we don't have to do everything by ourselves, but that we receive help, if our intentions are sincere.

In short, both from a psychological and a spiritual point of view, life flows better when we love. Therefore, the message of the Gospel about love, and the need to develop it, turns out to be a message of well-being. This message doesn't require us to associate love with suffering, but only with sacrifice, intended as *sacrum facere*, or sacral action.

From a strictly psychological point of view, we can even sacrifice our heart in favor of the mind, and after all we can function well enough yet, but certainly this cannot occur in the long run. A prolonged standing of life without love leads to emotional aridity and finally to a reduced mental functioning. Similarly, a psychological intervention that ignores the aspect of love becomes a psychologism, which risks of reinforce selfishness and an image of ourselves as omnipotent and self-sufficient.

Besides, from a spiritual point of view life doesn't flow at all and sooner or later it gets stuck, unless we make it receptive to the influence of the heart.

In order to heal our wounds, to accept and overcome our limits, we ultimately need to love. Of course, this must be a mature love as much as possible, also born from the belief that we must always look inside ourselves with clarity of purpose and with sincerity of mind, knowing that giving ourselves love without increasing the awareness of our mental processes could be useless and lead us to self-deception or to a self-consoling form, absolutely useless to our consciential growth.

In the first chapter I have talked about the structural limits and the ones produced by ourselves. In fact, we should try to accept the former, but we shouldn't indulge in the latter, on which we should work hard, however, especially with the tools provided by psychology. However, as I said earlier, not always psychology is the best cure to come out of narcissism, the major responsible for the self-produced limits. Sometimes, if psychology doesn't labor on the opening of the heart, it can create new and more dangerous defensive barriers in the person.

Via a suitable psychological intervention, we can also try to comprehend our omnipotent part that produces narcissistic factors, by loving it. Admittedly, this is paradoxical, because the self-produced limits derive from our psychological resistances and from our narcissism. How can we heal them with love if their intrinsic problem is essentially the lack of love?

This intervention can be done if we activate the will, that is a powerful tool for the psychological and spiritual synthesis, as it was shown by Assagioli. According to the great scholar, the integral will has three aspects: strength, goodness and wisdom.

Being strong, it guides the personal synthesis, helping to bring clarity in the incompleteness of the ego. Being good and wise, will is able to guide the person towards the realization of the highest motivations, operating a transpersonal psychosynthesis. Love is fundamental in these latter features.

It is clear that in order to overcome the limits self-produced by the mind, an intervention on a discomfort that has ontological roots is required. Among these there are the fear of death and the strong attachment to life, that is, some of those that have been described as human afflictions by Patanjali in the *Yogasutra*, the founding text of the *Yoga-darsana*.

These ontological factors are difficult to eradicate, and maybe we can't even think realistically to overcome them. However, we can work on them, in meditation or prayer (certainly not only via a conventional psychological work!)

It's the very fact of working on them, i.e., the attitude with which we try to face them, that creates in us a space of awareness and openness of heart. The hope that is activated by meditating or praying, and that almost automatically appears (unless we have strong resistances) when we seriously do this inner work, is itself a sign of openness of heart and makes us somehow taste how we could be and feel if we had an open heart. Both the sign and the real opening are two states of consciousness, the first one preparatory to the other one.

We may feel these states as temporary conditions or as ever more stable conditions. When they stabilize, they become stages of consciousness.

Of course, our ultimate goal in growing is to make the opening of the heart a stable event, but also enjoying this opening from time to time helps us in cultivating the certainty that it's possible to have a loving heart, and feel it deeply within us, even if we can't express it explicitly or we are stuck in its outward expression.

But, in and of itself, the fact of beginning to feel that within us there is something that vibrates, excites us and makes us feel alive, educates us and makes us feel certain that this is not an invention or something connected to a blind faith and scientifically unfounded.

This certainty, which begins in the heart and then goes to the head, causes that we learn to treat other people more kindly, though not indulgently. This second attitude may impede our riding the wave, because it feeds laziness and, in the long run, discouragement. Thus, without us realizing it, over time that hope loses its strenght, and we fall again in ordinariness, where the boundary between doing and not doing becomes very unstable. All this is worse than if we had cultivated only the deficiency motivations.

Being gentle with ourselves also means to have a look of benevolence towards ourselves when we have fallen prey to some narcissistic reaction, in which case we might get to thinking: "I won't change."

With regard to the attitude taken by a spiritual guide towards her disciple, a distinction must be drawn between the rigor required by an evolutionary path, where indulgence is not allowed in order not to give rise to narcissistic motivations, and the sternness arising instead from an internal request, corresponding to a rigid and hyper-requesting superego.

In the first case, the rigor is only meant to keep well delineated the boundary between truth and untruth and to correct any attempt aimed at diverting from truth. Such rigor doesn't create submission nor rebellion, unless the person interprets it as a superegoic voice and hasn't resolved the issues related to the conflict with the authority. It's the typical attitude taken by a guide who loves his disciple and cares about his destiny but is willing to wait for the disciple to understand by himself certain truths, being her only purpose the one to facilitate the disciple in recognizing the truth.

Besides, such an attitude doesn't create dependence; the disciple feels loved and understands the meaning of love, having experienced a selfless and high-quality love, the one transmitted by the guide.

The severity that comes from the superego, on the opposite, is highly detrimental, it creates in the disciple a hostile dependence, submission, forced condescension and, in the long run, a feeling of anger and rebellion. The superegoic attitude, harsh and malignant, present within oneself, causes an inner conflict very difficult to resolve, especially if it mixes with spiritual motivations. But it's even more dangerous if it is put in place unwittingly by the guide towards his disciple.

Therefore, the rebellion and the ensuing disobedience on the part of the disciple are a necessary consequence of a healthy defense put in action by him, who can no longer see – rightly – in his guide's attitudes disinterested corrections, meant to make truth while at the same time respecting the disciple's will and ability of vision, but only an inflated superego, convinced of its ideas.

These misunderstandings can cause a lot of pain in the disciples who walk with sincerity on a path of growth because, not perceiving fondness in their guide, but since they cannot conceive that their guide may put in place unconsciously the opposite of what she wants to convey, they are trapped in a sort of double bind in which, being unable to devalue the guide, they are inclined to sink into a pathological sense of guilt and to engage in a tougher job on their narcissism, that might be instead irrelevant.

While the disciple, if he succeeds in rebelling properly to an unfair and unaware treatment, moreover adopted from the one – the guide – who should teach him the exercise of awareness, is forced to continue his path and process a confusion not due to him, the guide often continues performing pretty much the same her task, convinced of the goodness of her work. Rather, the fact that the disciple has rebelled against her reinforces her conviction of having well wrought.

Unfortunately, it's very difficult that a spiritual guide gets herself really into question, recognizing her superegoic attitude (if any) as derived from her own egoic motivations; this shows how difficult it is to eradicate selfishness.

It's paradigmatic in this respect the self-denunciation made by Andrew Cohen, a well-known spiritual teacher, with many followers around the world. He announced in his blog, on June 26, 2013, that he wanted to take a sabbatical for an indefinite period, after he had had an intense confrontation with his closest disciples, who had helped him to realize, as he himself stated, that in spite of the depth of his spiritual awakening his ego was still alive and kicking.

About two years later, on May 12, 2015, Cohen posted a long letter of apology addressed to his former disciples. It was his first post since the beginning of his sabbatical retreat. He wrote on the need to embrace the spiritual principle of *agape* (love based on charity), in addition to that of *eros*, and he expressed regret about the ways in which his deficiency of agapic love in his teachings had wounded and pushed many of them away (source: wikipedia.org).

In his letter, Cohen acknowledged that, in the sincere attempt to reprimand his students, he had been too tough on them, excessively insisting on their narcissistic aspects without conveying love in his relationship with them, then resulting in an attitude of rebellion.

His refusal to recognize his disciples' feedbacks as coming from a healthy, and in many cases not narcissistic, psyche, caused him to capitulate at the end and to abandon his spiritual teaching, which he was being holding since thirty years.

Not being afraid to declare his narcissistic limits, he has shown a great courage and the truth that awareness is not a skill acquired once and for all, and the same holds for humility.

However, his self-criticism is admirable and even draws people near an idea of the spiritual guide that is more humane, limited and flawed; besides, it makes understand how the concept of spiritual "realization" or "liberation" is more a limit towards which to tend than a reality as widespread as one may think.

A spiritual guide is often idealized by her disciples, and this attitude denotes either the disciple's inability to experience love or an expectation that the guide fulfills totally their affective deficiencies.

Somehow, it is as if the disciple thought: "No one has loved me so far, because I have always met ordinary people; this guide is of the highest order, so she will surely love me and won't let me down."

This investment in terms of expectations on the figure of the guide, which is not required by her, necessarily leads to disappointment when the guide doesn't correspond to the excessive expectations. So, what should be a real love towards one's own guide proves to be a compensation, and this can affect the disciple's spiritual path, revealing his immaturity.

A similar relationship can be established in a spiritual brotherhood, with the brothers with whom one shares the common belonging to a path of transformation and evolution. This is the *philia*, that is, the fraternal love. However, since it is a matter of relationships among people who are full of incompleteness, if a bit of agape – the charitable love – doesn't flow in those relationships, one cannot overcome the critical moments occurring while sharing the same path.

Hence love, in its various forms, is a key ingredient in the relationships between human beings, especially among people who share a common purpose. Knowledge, which is necessary to evolve and grow in consciousness, is not sufficient in itself; it must be cultivated in a welcoming atmosphere, where love, sincere and disinterested as much as possible, can flow.

It is important that we spend time with people who love us. Of course, this doesn't mean that they should always agree with our choices.

This wouldn't really be evolutionary. We need people that reflect us in order to reveal parts of us that we don't want, or cannot, see. However, the feedbacks of people who don't love us, even if they are people with whom we share a path of growth, are useless to us; indeed, they equal to those of any stranger.

In a spiritual group, to prevent people from self-deceiving, a rule can be posed that every member ought to accept any feedback given by the brothers, provided those are loving feedbacks. If the feedbacks are judgments or, even worse, projections of one member onto the other, it's a responsibility of the guide leading the spiritual group to remind the correct mode of giving feedbacks. If she fails to do that, for instance, for fear of destabilizing the group, she commits a severe error and undermines the utility of giving feedbacks. In that case, the spiritual group may even risk involution.

Nobody needs people who give him feedbacks about his errors and limits in a cold and detached manner. Although the feedbacks can be true (partially or fully), they are doomed to generate a refusal on the part of the recipient, for the simple reason that no one ever needs to be treated harshly, if not the one who committed evil and shows no willingness to repent.

But a person who sins only by lack of awareness, being certainly wrong for this, and who apologizes for any faults she committed, is entitled to be treated with love, with a sincere and not falsely shown off love, at least just because God treats us lovingly, always and in any case. He doesn't punish us, but it's the laws of life that restore an order; these laws go under the name of *karma* in the Eastern tradition.

The person loving us gives us loving feedbacks; she doesn't linger in judgments, but tries to get into our motivations to understand them thoroughly, before she expresses an opinion, and she never feels entitled to have the last word.

If we believe in universal love, a love that transcends the egoic plan of life, we can develop empathy and comprehension of the other, arising from an attitude of love and respect, as well as compassion.

While we ride the wave, we are halfway between the ego and the Self; we have not yet overcome entirely the deficiency needs but we are open to a higher dimension, that the limits of our ego prevent us from reaching easily. In this context, love turns out to be the most powerful means to accept the ego as it is and to open our heart to the influence of the Self.

Then, the new desire for freedom that our ego feels is called to be transformed into a desire for the Absolute, which is probably the most authentic and truest need of the human being, of *every* human being.

www.ingramcontent.com/pod-product-compliance
Lightning Source LLC
Chambersburg PA
CBHW030443290526
45786CB00001B/426